STORIES FROM AFRICA

40 Folktales of the Motherland from The Diaspora

Ali Abdael

TABLE OF CONTENTS

INTRODUCTION

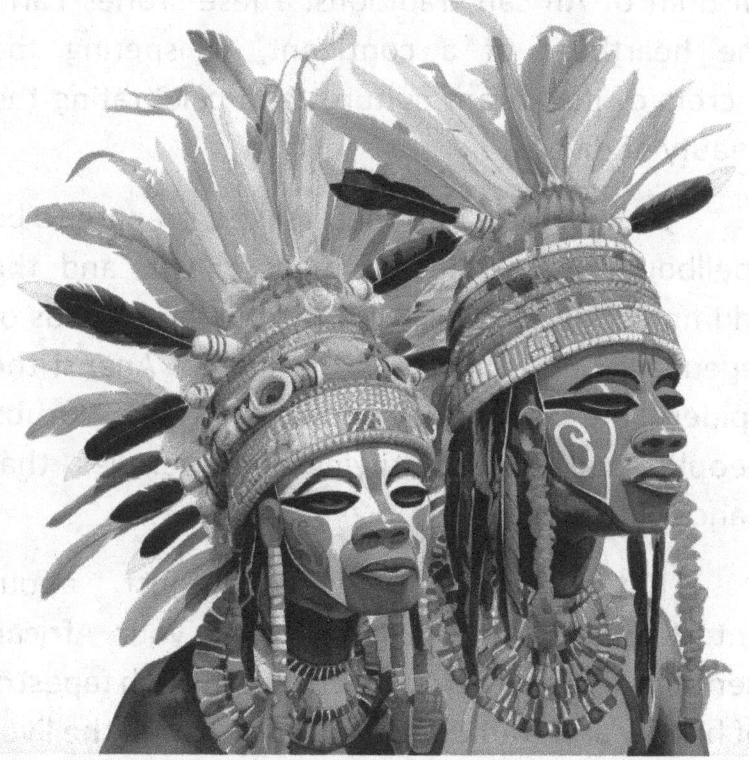

Welcome, young explorers, to a world filled with wonder, magic, and ancient tales that have traveled across generations! In this book, we invite you to embark on an extraordinary journey through the enchanting lands of Africa, where captivating folklore stories come alive.

With every turn of the page, you'll discover a tapestry woven with colorful characters, brave heroes, mischievous creatures, and the timeless wisdom of African traditions. These stories carry the heartbeat of a continent, whispering the secrets of its vibrant cultures and celebrating the beauty of diversity.

As you delve into these pages, prepare to be spellbound by stories of bravery, wit, and the triumph of good over evil. Uncover the legends of legendary beings, such as the mighty Anansi the Spider, the fascinating deities of the Yoruba people, and the mystifying masquerades that dance with joy.

But this book is not just about entertainment. It is a gateway to your African heritage, a chance to connect with the rich tapestry of history and traditions that have shaped the lives of countless generations. It is a celebration of your roots, inviting you to embrace the beauty and strength of Africa's past, present, and future.

So, young readers, get ready to embark on an unforgettable adventure. Open your minds and hearts as we traverse the vast savannas, lush forests, and bustling marketplaces of Africa. Let your imagination soar as we meet clever tricksters, powerful spirits, and ordinary people who rise to extraordinary heights.

Are you ready? Then let's begin this magical journey and uncover the treasures that lie within the captivating African folklore!

ANANSI THE CLEVER SPIDER (GHANA)

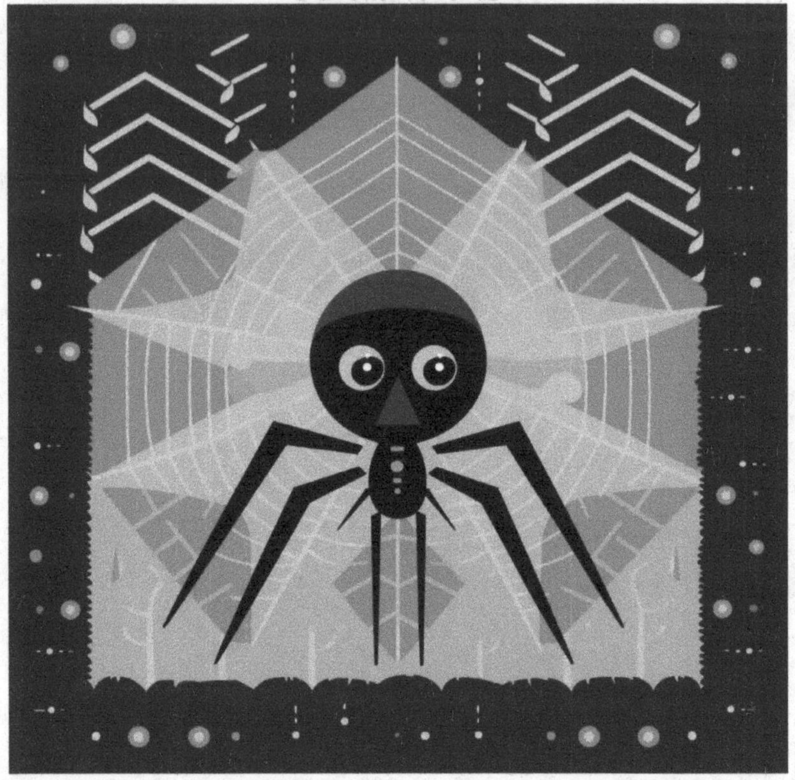

Once upon a time, in a beautiful African forest, there lived a mischievous and clever spider named Anansi. Anansi was known far and wide for his quick wit and cunning ways. He had a shiny black body, long spindly legs, and eyes that twinkled mischievously. Anansi loved to explore and discover new things, and his adventures were the talk of the forest.

Now, the reason why Anansi is so popular is because he always outsmarts even the trickiest of situations. He would weave elaborate webs to catch delicious insects and spin intricate tales to outsmart his friends. But Anansi's cleverness didn't end there. He could even fool the powerful animals of the forest, like the mighty elephant and the fierce lion.

Kids, imagine being as clever as Anansi! Picture yourself joining him on his exciting escapades, swinging from branch to branch, and unraveling mysteries of the forest. Together with Anansi, you'll encounter talking animals, navigate treacherous paths, and face thrilling challenges that require your wits and bravery. Now to the story...

In the heart of a bustling African village in Ghana, nestled under the shade of a majestic baobab tree, lived a spider named Anansi. With eight spindly legs and eyes that gleamed like tiny stars, Anansi was not your ordinary arachnid. He was a master weaver, storyteller, and the cleverest creature in all the land.

One sunny day, the animals of the village gathered in the clearing, eager to hear another of Anansi's legendary tales. Anansi, perched on a silken thread, cleared his throat and began to weave a web of enchantment with his words.

"Once upon a time," Anansi began, "the sun and the moon decided to have a contest to determine who was the most powerful." The animals leaned in, captivated by Anansi's voice as it danced through the air.

"The sun, proud and bright, declared, 'I am the ruler of the day! No one can shine as brilliantly as I do!'" Anansi's voice rose and fell, mimicking the sun's grandeur.

"But the moon, calm and serene, replied, 'Ah, but I bring light to the night when darkness descends. My glow guides weary travelers and fills the sky with mystery.'"

The animals listened in awe as Anansi skillfully spun the tale of how the sun and the moon went on a quest to find the wise old Sky God, Nyame, to settle their dispute. Anansi, always a step ahead, devised a plan to outsmart the celestial beings and claim a reward for himself.

Through a series of clever tricks and cunning disguises, Anansi convinced the Sky God that he could gather all the wisdom in the world and store it in a magical gourd. Nyame, impressed by Anansi's boldness, granted him the gift of storytelling and wisdom.

With his newfound wisdom, Anansi returned to the village and shared his tales with the animals. Each story carried a valuable lesson, teaching the importance of bravery, kindness, and quick thinking. The animals marveled at Anansi's ability to turn the ordinary into the extraordinary, and they couldn't wait for the next chapter of his adventures.

As Anansi's tales spread throughout the land, children from the African diaspora, eager to connect with their heritage, would gather around their elders to hear the marvelous stories of the clever spider. They would learn about the rich tapestry of African traditions, values, and the wisdom passed down through generations.

So, my young friends, let Anansi's web of wisdom and his mischievous spirit inspire you. Learn from his cleverness, bravery, and the power of a well-told story. Together, we shall journey into the heart of African folklore, unlocking the magic that lies within and connecting with our roots in a truly captivating way.

Lessons

* Anansi's tricks often taught important lessons, like the value of using your brains instead of your brawn.

*His stories also carried messages about fairness, kindness, and the consequences of greed.

*Through his tales, children could learn to think creatively, solve problems, and be wise in their decision-making.

THE CREATION OF THE WORLD (DEMOCRATIC REPUBLIC OF THE CONGO)

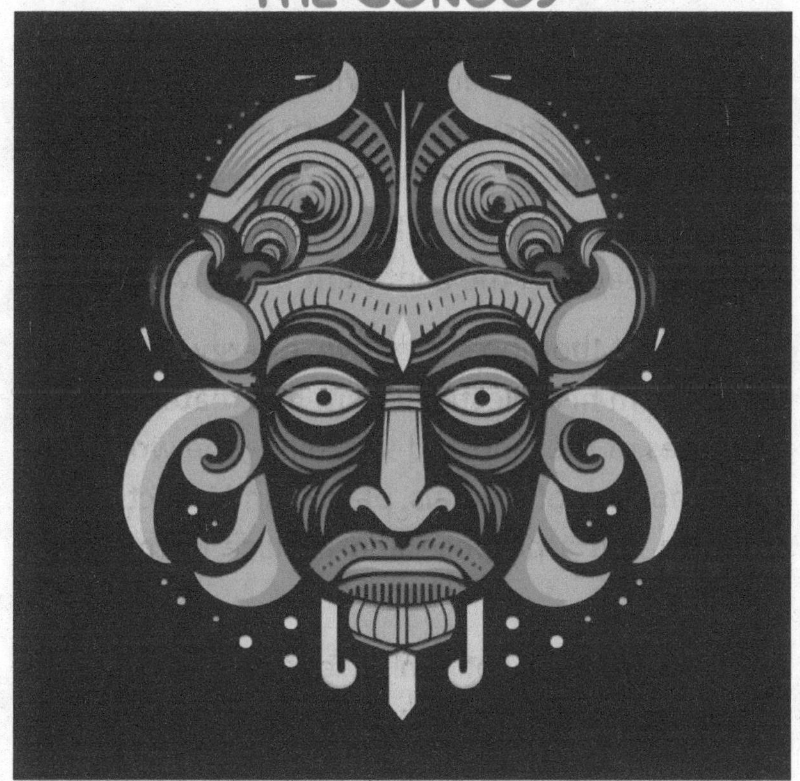

Once upon a time, in the vast and vibrant continent of Africa, the gods gathered together, each possessing a unique talent and purpose. There was Mbombo, the Creator, who was surrounded by a swirling, cosmic soup of colors. Mbombo held within him the essence of life, and as he stirred this celestial mixture, he began to vomit out the sun, the moon, the stars, and all the wonders of the universe.

As Mbombo continued to bring forth creation, he felt a sudden urge to unleash his power in a mighty burst. With an explosion that shook the heavens and the earth, Mbombo hurled forth mountains, valleys, and mighty oceans. The ground quaked, and the land split open, revealing the vast beauty of the continent we now call Africa.

But Mbombo's creative energy didn't end there. From his celestial vomit, he created the first creatures of the land and sea, filling the world with a rich tapestry of animals, plants, and insects. Every creature had a purpose and a place in this grand design.

As the story of "The Creation of the World" has been passed down through generations, it has become a cherished tale, treasured for its profound significance. The Kuba people of Central Africa, in the territory now known as the Democratic Republic of the Congo, worship Mbombo, also called Bumba, as their creator god in their religion and mythology. Mbombo was described as a white giant in the Mbombo creation tale. The myth explains how the universe came into being out of nothing.

<u>**Lessons**</u>

*"The Creation of the World" serves as a precious link to their African heritage. It allows them to understand their roots, to feel a sense of pride in their ancestry, and to appreciate the wonders of the natural world.

*This folklore reminds us that we are all connected, part of a magnificent tapestry woven by the gods.

*It teaches us to appreciate the beauty and diversity of the world around us and to respect and care for the delicate balance of nature.

<u>Lessons</u>

THE LEGEND OF OSUN: THE RIVER GODDESS (YORUBA. NIGERIA)

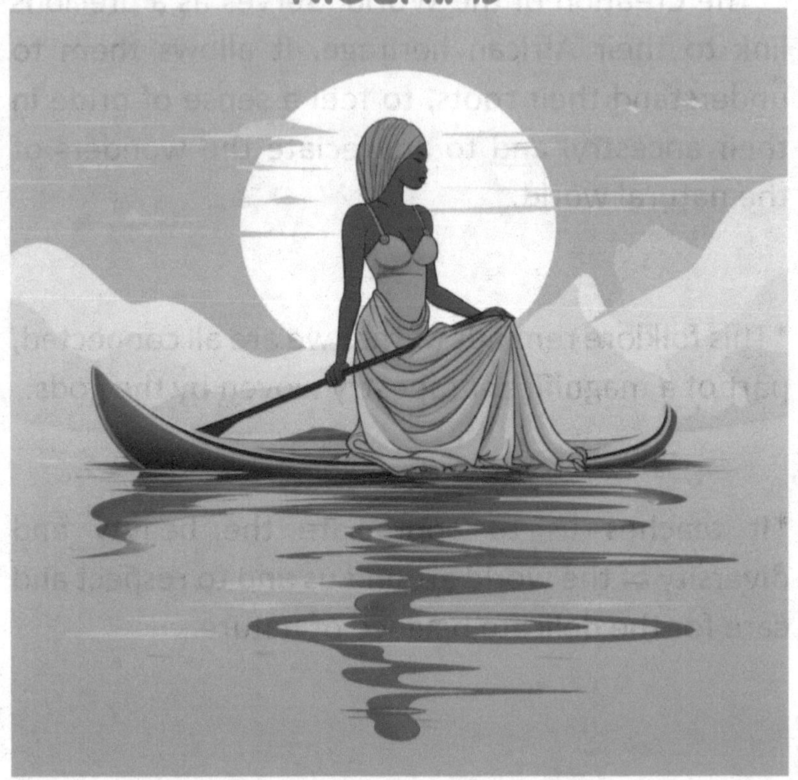

Once upon a time, in a land filled with lush forests and sparkling rivers, there lived a wise and beautiful goddess named Osun. Her radiant smile could brighten the darkest of days, and her magical powers were renowned throughout the Yoruba kingdom of Nigeria. The Legend of Osun is a tale that has captivated hearts for generations, and its significance holds a special place in African folklore.

Osun was not just any ordinary goddess; she was the protector of the rivers, the goddess of love and fertility, and the bringer of healing and prosperity. People believed that her presence brought harmony to their lives, and they would often visit her sacred groves to seek her blessings. The legend tells of a time when the land faced a terrible drought, and the crops withered, leaving the people in despair.

One day, a young girl named Adeola ventured deep into the forest in search of a remedy for her village's plight. As she wandered through the trees, she stumbled upon a hidden waterfall, where a shimmering figure emerged from the waters. It was Osun herself, with her golden crown and flowing robes.

In her gentle voice, Osun asked Adeola why she had come. The young girl tearfully explained the suffering her village endured due to the drought.

Touched by Adeola's sincerity, Osun decided to help. She taught Adeola the secret songs and dances that would please the spirits of the rivers and bring rain to the land.

Adeola returned to her village, spreading Osun's teachings and encouraging everyone to join in the celebration. The villagers sang and danced, their voices echoing through the valleys, and their feet creating rhythmic beats on the earth. Their devotion touched Osun's heart, and as the last notes of their songs filled the air, rain began to fall gently from the sky.

Today, the Yoruba people still celebrate Osun's legacy through vibrant festivals and ceremonies. They decorate her statues with colorful beads, sing her praises, and offer gifts in gratitude for her blessings. It is a beautiful tradition that connects generations, ensuring that the magic of Osun's legend lives on.

<u>Lessons</u>

*The Legend of Osun became popular because it symbolizes the power of nature, the importance of community, and the belief in the supernatural.

*It teaches us that with faith, unity, and respect for the environment, we can overcome even the most challenging times.

*Osun's story reminds us to cherish and protect our natural resources, for they are the key to our survival and prosperity.

THE STORY OF THE COURAGEOUS LION KING- SUNDIATA (MANDINKA. MALI)

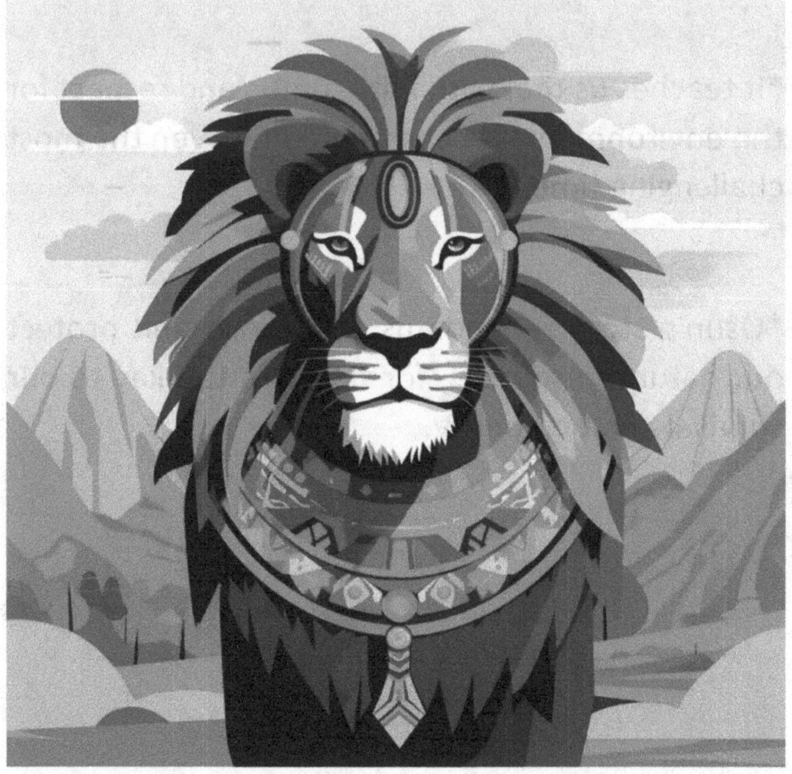

Once upon a time, in the magnificent land of Mali, there lived a young prince named Sundiata. He was no ordinary prince; he possessed strength, wisdom, and a heart filled with bravery. But there was something extraordinary about Sundiata—he was bound to become a legendary king!

The Epic of Sundiata is a story that has been passed down through generations, capturing the hearts and minds of people across Africa. It tells the incredible tale of a young hero overcoming great obstacles to fulfill his destiny and bring peace to his kingdom.

Sundiata was born to the noble Keita family, but due to a cruel twist of fate, he was unable to walk. However, this did not dampen his spirit. With the support of his loyal friends and the guidance of his mother, Sogolon, who possessed mystical powers, Sundiata embarked on a remarkable journey.

As Sundiata grew older, he discovered his immense strength and his ability to communicate with animals. One day, he encountered a majestic lion who recognized his true potential and became his loyal companion. Together, they formed an unbreakable bond, protecting each other through thick and thin.

But Sundiata's journey was not an easy one. He faced a powerful sorcerer named Soumaoro, who ruled Mali with an iron fist. Soumaoro was feared by all, but Sundiata's determination and unwavering courage could not be shaken. With his loyal friends by his side and the wisdom of his ancestors guiding him, Sundiata set out to defeat the sorcerer and liberate his people.

Through this captivating tale, kids like you can connect with their African roots and be inspired by the strength and resilience of their ancestors. So join Sundiata on his extraordinary quest, where you'll witness breathtaking battles, encounter magical creatures, and learn invaluable lessons about the true meaning of heroism.

Lessons

*The Epic of Sundiata teaches us the importance of perseverance, bravery, and the power of unity.

*Sundiata's story is a symbol of hope and triumph, reminding us that no obstacle is insurmountable when we believe in ourselves and stand together.

THE COW-TAIL SWITCH
(LIBERIA)

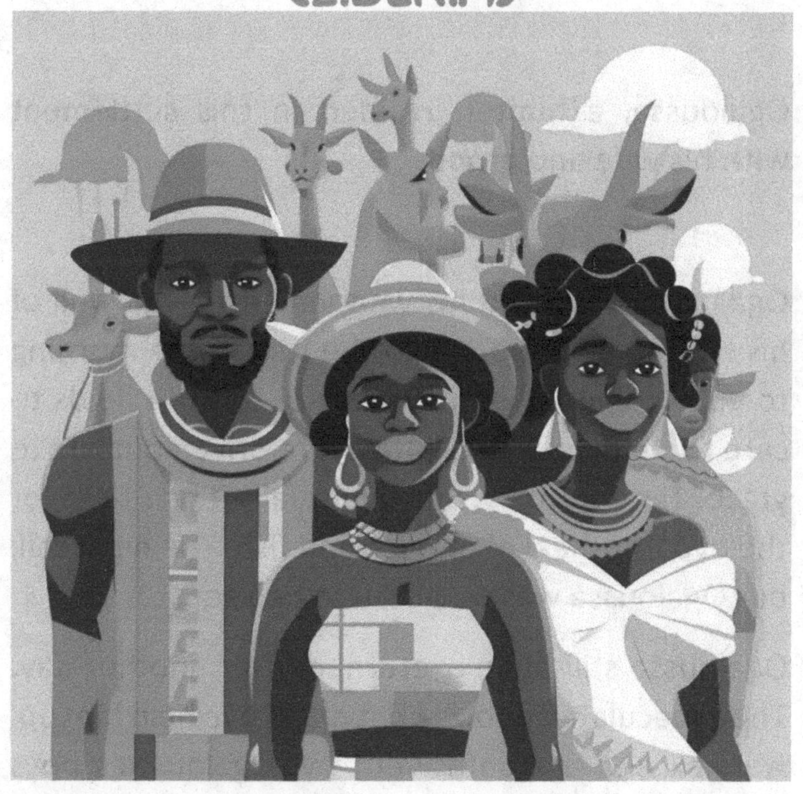

Kundi was a small Liberian community located on a hill above the Cavally River, not far from the forest's border. All around it are rice and cassava farms. In the meadow beside the river, cattle grazed. From afar, thin columns of smoke emanating from the fires in the circular clay cottages could be seen to float over the settlement. Women pounded grain in wooden mortars outside their homes while their husbands and sons fished in the river with nets.

Ogaloussa, a hunter, resided in this settlement with his wife and brood.

Ogaloussa retrieved his weapons from the wall of his home and set out into the forest one morning to go hunting. His family went out to the fields to care to them, and the cattle were driven outside to graze. Time went by, and eventually it was time for the evening meal of manioc and fish. The night fell, but Ogaloussa was nowhere to be seen.

Ogaloussa still hadn't returned after another day. They speculated about what may have held him up. A week and a month went by. Ogaloussa's boys would sometimes suggest that Dad hadn't returned home. After a time, the family stopped discussing Ogaloussa's departure and focused instead on caring for the crops and hunting for food with the boys.

Then, one day, Ogaloussa's wife gave birth to a second son. Puli was his name. Age crept up on

Puli. The first thing he uttered after opening his mouth was, "Where is my father?"

The other boys surveyed the vast expanse of rice fields.

"Yes," one of them said. To which one may ask, "Where is father?"

Another said, "He really should have come back a long time ago."

Clearly something has transpired. A third child suggested that "we should look for him."

"He went into the forest, but where will we find him?" another questioned.

One of them added, "I saw him leave." He crossed the river and headed in that direction. Let's look for him by following the clues.

The boys armed themselves and set out to find their missing father, Ogaloussa. In the thick of the forest's towering trees and sprawling vines, they lost the path. In the woods, they looked for it until one of them came across it again. They followed it until they got lost again, and then one of the sons rediscovered it. It was late, and the jungle was dense enough that they often missed their way. Another son would eventually figure it out. Finally they reached an open area amid the woods, and there Ogaloussa's bones and rusting weaponry were strewn around. Ogaloussa's death in the search was confirmed at that time.

One of the boys spoke out, proclaiming, "I know how to put a dead person's bones together." He collected all of Ogaloussa's bones and carefully reassembled him.

A second child chimed in, "I know stuff, too. I'm an expert at putting skin and muscle on a skeleton. While away at work, he attached muscle and fat to Ogaloussa's skeleton.

In the words of a third child: "I have the power to put blood into a body." He then left the room after injecting blood into Ogaloussa's veins.

In the words of one of the sons: "I can put breath into a body." He finished his task, and everyone could see Ogaloussa's chest move up and down as a result.

Another added, "I can give the power of movement to a body." He willed his father to sit up and open his eyes, and Ogaloussa responded.

"I can give him the power of speech," another son said. Then he backed off after giving the body the ability to speak.

Ogaloussa scanned the area. He got to his feet.

He enquired, "Where are my weapons?"

His rusty weapons were retrieved from the ground and returned to him. They turned around and made their way back through the woods and the rice paddies to the settlement.

When Ogaloussa got home, he went inside. His wife ran him a bath and he relaxed in it. She cooked for him, and he dined. After staying indoors for four days, he shaved his head on the fifth day in accordance with the customs of those who had just returned from the afterlife.

He then slaughtered a cow for a massive feast. He plaited a braid out of the cow's tail. Beads, cowry shells, and glints of metal were among the embellishments he added. In a word, it was stunning. Ogaloussa often took it with him when he had to attend a formal event. He never left home without it for a ball or formal event. The villagers unanimously agreed that it was the most stunning example of a cow-tail switch they had ever seen.

Ogaloussa's resurrection prompted immediate celebrations in the town. Everyone put on their finest attire, the band struck up, and the dance party got under way. Women sang while drums pounded in the background. Lots of palm wine was consumed by the crowd. There was joy all around.

Ogaloussa always had his cow-tail switch on him, and it was a sight to see. Braver than before, several of the guys approached Ogaloussa and demanded the cow-tail switch, but Ogaloussa held on to it. Every once in a while, there would be a commotion and a lot of confusion as a lot of people would all want it at once. The ladies and children also pleaded, but Ogaloussa would have none of it.

At last, he got up to address the crowd. People stopped dancing and gathered around Ogaloussa to listen to him.

"I went into the forest a very long time ago," Ogaloussa recalled. I was hunting when I was attacked by a leopard. After that, my kids came to get me. They raised me from the grave, but I only have one cow tail to share. I'm going to give it to the person who was most instrumental in getting me back.

An altercation ensued as a result.

One of the sons said, "He will give it to me!" When the route got lost in the woods, it was I who discovered it.

The response was emphatic: "No, he will give it to me!" a second son added. I assembled his skeleton, so to speak.

Another chimed in, "It was I who covered his bones with sinews and flesh!" "He's gonna hand it over to me!"

Another son exclaimed, "It was I who gave him the power of movement!" I am the one who is due the greatest praise.

He who injected blood into Ogaloussa's veins, said another son, should be the one to flip the switch. The person who breathed life into the corpse staked his claim to it. The three brothers battled about who should keep the priceless cow-tail switch.

The sons started conversing, and soon the rest of the villagers joined in. Some said the son who gave Ogaloussa life should have the power, while others said the son who gave him blood should. There were many who argued that the sons should divide the inheritance evenly since they had all contributed equally. This went on until Ogaloussa finally begged them to stop.

Because he is the one to whom Ogaloussa owes the most, this son will get the cow-tail switch.

He stepped forward, placed a little wager, and gave the money to Puli, the baby born while Ogaloussa was in the woods.

After hearing the child's first words, the villagers recalled their first reaction: "Where is my father?" That Ogaloussa was correct was obvious to them.

For among them there circulated the proverb that one is not really dead until he is forgotten.

Lessons

* The story teaches the moral that knowledge is better than pure strength.

* Another moral of the story is that a person is never really dead, until he is forgotten.

THE MAGIC CALABASH (ZULU. SOUTH AFRICA)

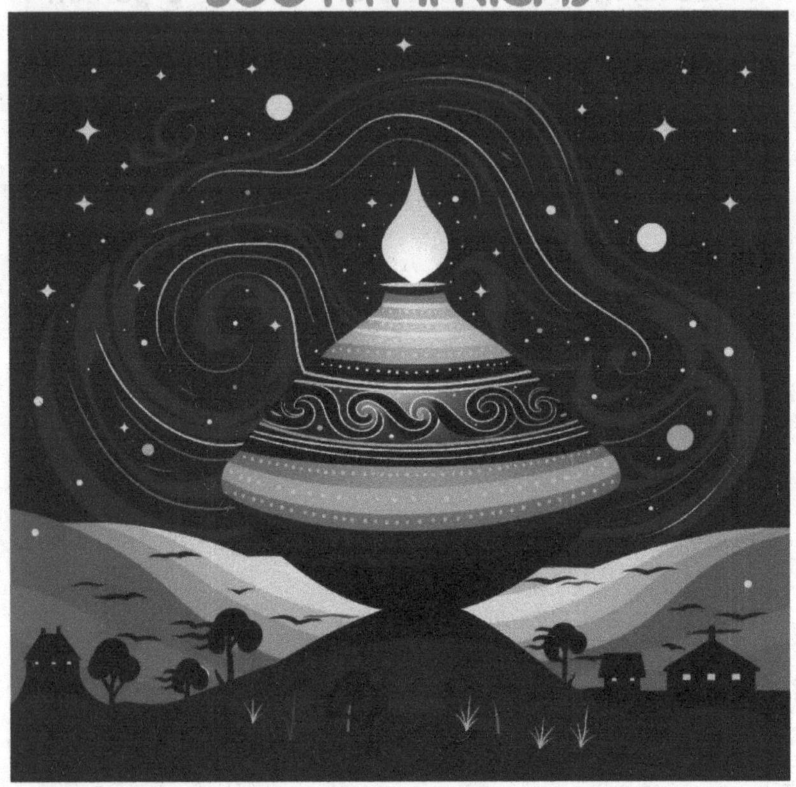

Once upon a time, in the enchanting lands of South Africa, there existed a legendary tale known as "The Magic Calabash." This captivating story has been passed down from generation to generation among the Zulu people, filling their hearts with wonder and excitement.

Picture a vibrant village nestled amidst rolling hills and lush greenery. In this village lived a young boy named Sipho. Sipho had always been curious and adventurous, seeking thrilling tales that would transport him to magical realms. One day, as he roamed the outskirts of his village, he stumbled upon a hidden treasure—the Magic Calabash.

The Magic Calabash was no ordinary gourd. It shimmered and glowed with an ethereal light, as if touched by the heavens themselves. Legend had it that this calabash possessed extraordinary powers, capable of granting the wishes of those who treated it with respect and kindness.

Eager to uncover the truth behind the legends, Sipho carefully picked up the Magic Calabash. As he did, a gentle whisper filled the air, beckoning him to embark on a thrilling journey. With eyes wide with anticipation, Sipho clutched the calabash tightly and whispered his heart's desire—a chance to discover the hidden wonders of his ancestors' land.

In an instant, the Magic Calabash whisked Sipho away, soaring through the sky like a shooting star. They journeyed over vast savannahs, majestic mountains, and sparkling rivers. Sipho marveled at the breathtaking sights, feeling his heart fill with a profound sense of belonging and pride.

As they descended to a bustling marketplace, Sipho noticed vibrant colors and the joyous sound of drums filling the air. People from all walks of life were gathered, dressed in magnificent traditional attire. Sipho had arrived at the heart of a Zulu celebration—a festival that honored their culture, customs, and the spirit of togetherness.

The Magic Calabash led Sipho through the crowd, where he encountered masquerades adorned in dazzling costumes, dancing gracefully to the rhythmic beats of the drums. Their vibrant masks whispered tales of bravery, wisdom, and mythical creatures. Sipho couldn't help but dance along, feeling the rhythm pulsate through his veins.

As night fell, a bonfire was lit, casting flickering shadows on the faces of the villagers. Elders gathered around, their voices rising in harmony as they shared ancient stories of heroes and heroines, of mighty warriors and wise queens. Sipho listened with awe, captivated by each word that transported him to a time long ago.

The Magic Calabash ensured that Sipho experienced the very essence of Zulu traditions and the significance of honoring their heritage. It taught him the importance of unity, respect, and cherishing the stories passed down by their ancestors. With newfound knowledge and a heart filled with pride, Sipho returned home, forever changed.

Lessons

*The tale of the Magic Calabash inspires all to embrace their African roots, no matter where they may reside.

*This tale is a reminder of their vibrant heritage and the boundless possibilities that lie within.

THE TORTOISE AND THE BIRDS (IGBO, NIGERIA)

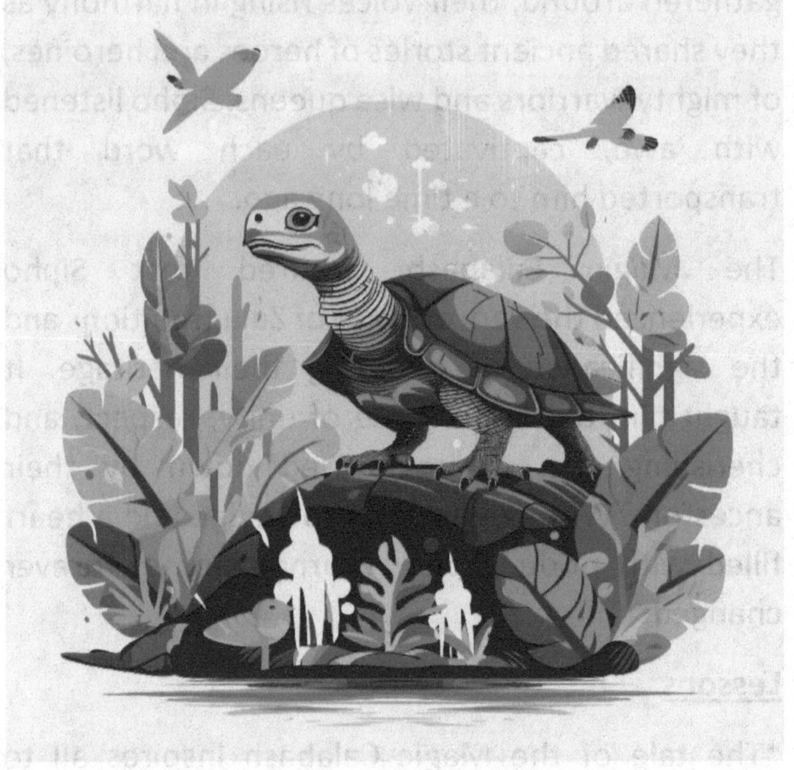

Once upon a time, in a lush land of vibrant colors and rolling hills, there lived a mischievous and cunning Tortoise. He was known far and wide for his cleverness and his ability to outwit even the craftiest of creatures. One sunny day, the Tortoise hatched a devious plan that would forever be etched in the annals of Igbo folklore.

Now, nestled high up in the branches of the mighty Iroko tree were a community of beautiful, melodious birds. Their feathers shimmered in all shades of the rainbow, and their songs filled the air with joy. They were guardians of the skies, soaring through the heavens with grace and elegance.

But the Tortoise, oh how he coveted their freedom! He longed to experience the exhilaration of flight, to feel the wind rush through his shell as he soared above the treetops. And so, he concocted a scheme to trick the birds into sharing their secret.

With a sly smile on his face, the Tortoise made his way to the foot of the Iroko tree. He looked up at the birds and called out to them in his most polite and persuasive voice, "Dear birds, I have heard tales of your marvelous ability to fly. How I wish to witness the world from your lofty heights! Might you consider teaching me your wondrous art?"

The birds, captivated by the Tortoise's words, gathered together to discuss this unexpected request. They marveled at the audacity of the Tortoise's desire. "How could a creature with such a heavy shell ever dream of soaring through the sky?" they wondered. Nevertheless, they saw no harm in sharing their gift, for birds are known for their kindness and generosity.

And so, the birds huddled close, whispering secrets and formulating a plan. They agreed to fashion a set of feathered wings for the Tortoise, so he too could experience the wonders of flight. With great care, they wove delicate strands of colorful feathers into a magnificent pair of wings.

Excitement filled the air as the Tortoise donned his newfound wings. With a newfound sense of freedom and exhilaration, he flapped his wings with all his might, attempting to take flight. But alas, his heavy shell weighed him down, and he only managed to flap his wings feebly.

The birds, overcome with laughter, realized the Tortoise had played a trick on them. They had underestimated his cunning ways. The Tortoise, undeterred by his failed attempt, simply smiled. He had achieved his true goal: to remind the birds of their own unique gift, the ability to soar effortlessly through the skies.

Dear young readers, let this tale inspire you to embrace your own unique qualities and talents. Just as the Tortoise and the birds learned from their encounter, may you remember that diversity is a beautiful tapestry that enriches our world. So spread your wings, metaphorical or otherwise, and let your imagination soar, for within each of you lies a spark of greatness waiting to be discovered.

Lessons

*The Tortoise and the Birds serves as a cautionary reminder of the dangers of pride and the importance of embracing one's own strengths and gifts.

*The story teaches us that each creature possesses their own special abilities, and it is when we appreciate and celebrate these differences that true harmony is achieved.

THE ORISHAS AND THEIR POWERS (YORUBA, NIGERIA)

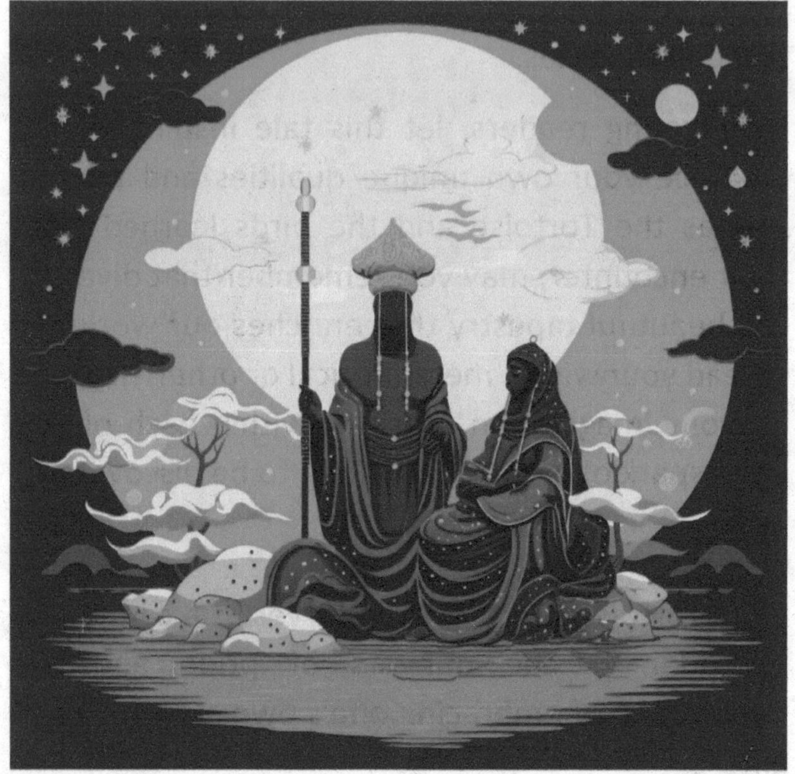

Once upon a time, in the ancient land of Nigeria, there existed a mystical realm filled with powerful beings called the Orishas. These extraordinary creatures were revered by the Yoruba people, who believed that they possessed incredible powers and held sway over various aspects of the world.

Let me take you on a thrilling journey through the captivating world of the Orishas and their Powers. Imagine a realm where the wind whispers secrets, where the rivers flow with wisdom, and where the sun dances with joy. In this enchanting land, the Orishas ruled with grace and strength, guiding the destiny of humanity.

First, there was Ogun, the mighty warrior Orisha. With his sturdy frame and gleaming sword, Ogun protected the people from harm and taught them the art of forging weapons. His strength and courage were legendary, and his presence instilled bravery in the hearts of all.

Next, there was Yemoja, the gentle and nurturing Orisha of the oceans. Imagine vast waves crashing against the shores, carrying the hopes and dreams of sailors and fishermen. Yemoja, with her motherly embrace, ensured the safety of those who ventured into her watery domain. She watched over them, guiding their vessels and providing bountiful catches.

Obatala, the wise and creative Orisha, stood tall in his resplendent white robes. He possessed the power to shape clay into marvelous sculptures, bringing beauty and harmony into the world. Obatala inspired artists and craftsmen, urging them to explore the depths of their imagination and create wonders that would dazzle the eye.

In the vibrant tapestry of Yoruba folklore, Sango, the tempestuous Orisha of thunder and lightning, roared with his mighty voice and shook the heavens. He commanded the elements and unleashed bolts of lightning across the sky, reminding the people of the awesome power of nature. Sango's presence reminded them to respect the forces of the world and find strength within themselves.

Oshun, the captivating Orisha of love and beauty, graced the land with her radiant smile and gentle laughter. She danced gracefully along the rivers, her golden dress shimmering in the sunlight. Oshun filled the world with joy, inspiring poets and musicians, and teaching the people to find love and happiness in every moment.

Finally, we come to Eshu, the mischievous trickster Orisha. Eshu was known for his cunning and cleverness. He delighted in playing pranks on both humans and fellow Orishas, but his antics always carried a deeper meaning. Eshu taught important lessons about the consequences of our actions, reminding us to think before we act and consider the impact on others.

The Orishas and their Powers hold a significant place in Yoruba culture. So, dear young adventurers, let your imagination soar as you explore the realm of the Orishas and their Powers. Remember that within each of you lies the potential for greatness, just like these extraordinary beings. Embrace your heritage and let the wisdom of the Orishas guide you on your own magical journey of self-discovery and understanding.

Lessons

*The Orishas teach us about courage, nurturing, creativity, strength, love, and the importance of balance.

*Through their stories, we learn to embrace our own unique qualities and appreciate the diverse powers that exist within us and the world around us.

THE LION'S WHISKER (ETHIOPIA)

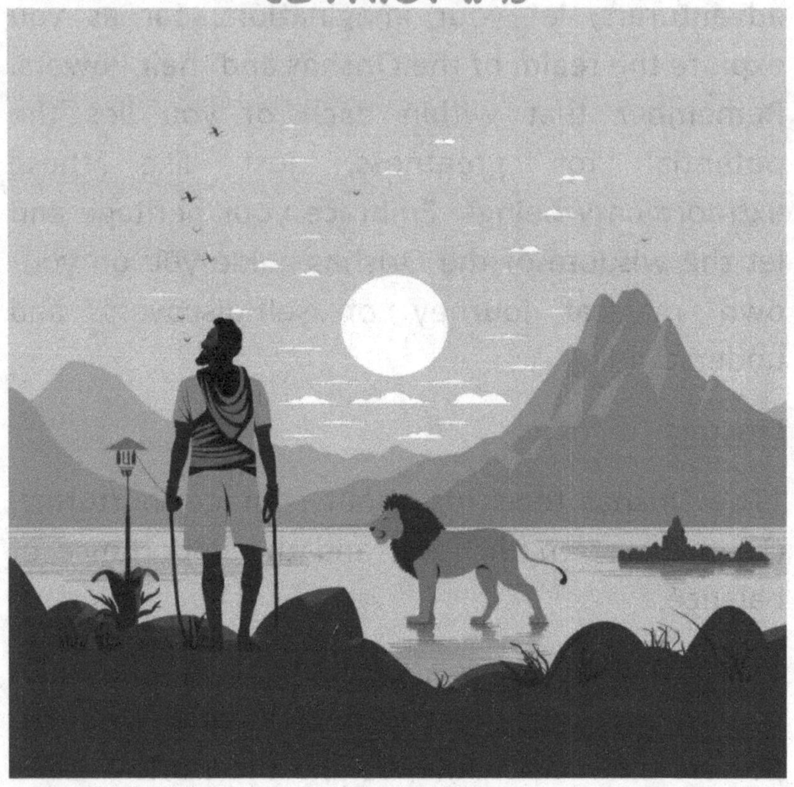

Once upon a time, in the vast plains of Ethiopia, there lived a wise old lion. This lion was known for his majestic golden mane that shimmered under the warm African sun. But there was something more extraordinary about this lion than just his appearance. He possessed a secret power, hidden within the whiskers that adorned his mighty face.

Now, children, close your eyes and imagine the breathtaking beauty of the Ethiopian landscape. Picture the tall grasses swaying gently in the wind, as the lion roamed freely in search of his next meal. But, as clever as he was, he knew that in order to survive, he needed more than just strength and speed. He needed wisdom.

One day, news reached the lion's ears of a great challenge that had befallen the animal kingdom. A terrible sickness had swept across the land, leaving the creatures weak and helpless. Even the mightiest of lions and the swiftest of antelopes had succumbed to this mysterious ailment. Desperate for a solution, they sought the lion's counsel.

Deep in thought, the lion ventured to the heart of the enchanted forest, where the wise old owl lived. The owl was renowned for his knowledge of ancient remedies and his ability to unravel the secrets of nature. With hope in his heart, the lion presented himself before the owl and shared the plight of his fellow animals.

The wise owl listened intently, his bright eyes twinkling with wisdom. After a moment of contemplation, he revealed a secret to the lion—a magical plant hidden deep within the forest. This plant possessed the power to heal any ailment, but its location remained a mystery. The only clue was that it could only be found with the help of a single lion's whisker.

Eager to help his animal friends, the lion embarked on a treacherous journey, navigating through dense jungles and climbing treacherous cliffs. He faced roaring rivers and confronted formidable predators, all in search of this mystical plant. But the real challenge lay within himself. He had to summon the courage to pluck one of his precious whiskers and sacrifice it for the greater good.

Finally, after days of relentless pursuit, the lion discovered the hidden plant, glowing with an otherworldly radiance. With trembling paws, he plucked a whisker from his regal mane and gently touched it to the leaves of the plant. A powerful energy surged through his body, infusing him with strength and healing.

Returning triumphantly to the animal kingdom, the lion shared the magical plant's essence, curing every creature that was suffering. The animals marveled at his selflessness and bravery, forever grateful for the lion's sacrifice. From that day forward, the lion's whisker became a symbol of wisdom, healing, and the importance of helping others in times of need.

<u>**Lessons**</u>

*The story of the Lion's Whisker from Ethiopia teaches us about the incredible power of compassion, courage, and sacrifice.

*It reminds us to look beyond our own needs and lend a helping hand to those around us.

*Just like the lion, let us be brave, wise, and always ready to make a difference in the world.

WHY THE SUN AND THE MOON LIVE IN THE SKY (NIGERIA)

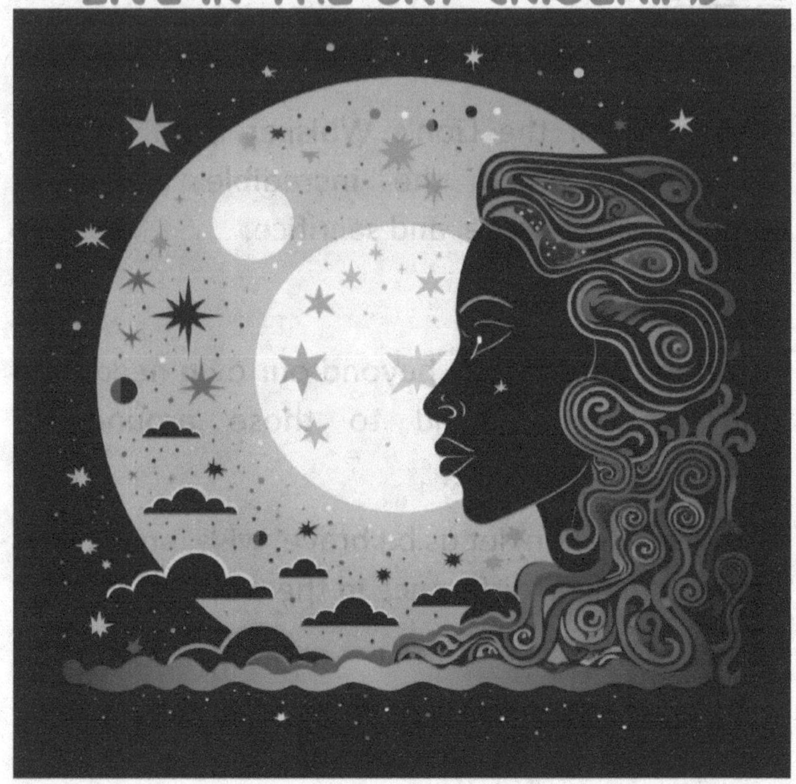

In a tiny village somewhere in Nigeria; nestled amidst rolling hills and shimmering rivers, there resided a mischievous and curious little boy named Kofi. Kofi loved to explore the depths of the lush forests and play with the animals that called the land their home.

One sunny day, as Kofi ventured deeper into the woods, he stumbled upon a magical clearing. It was as if the air crackled with a sense of mystery and wonder. Within this enchanted glade, Kofi discovered a gathering of animals, all chattering excitedly.

At the center of the assembly stood the wise old Tortoise, who carried an air of great importance. "My dear friends," he began, "we must solve the problem that plagues our land. You see, the Sun and the Moon used to live among us, bringing warmth and light to our days and nights. But now, they reside high above in the sky, and we are left in darkness."

Intrigued, Kofi listened closely, his eyes wide with anticipation. The Tortoise continued, "Long ago, the Sun and the Moon were married, radiating joy and light upon the Earth. However, their harmony was disrupted by a terrible argument. The Sun claimed to be the greatest light in the world, while the Moon argued that her gentle glow was just as important."

The animals exchanged concerned glances, wondering how this dispute could be resolved. The

Tortoise, known for his wisdom, proposed a plan. "Let us summon the Sun and the Moon and remind them of their true purpose—to illuminate our world with their combined brilliance."

Eager to play a part in this quest, Kofi and the animals embarked on a daring adventure. They traveled far and wide, seeking the guidance of the wise Oracle, an ancient and revered figure. The Oracle shared her wisdom, instructing them to bring the Sun and the Moon back together in the spirit of unity.

Armed with hope and determination, Kofi and his newfound animal friends set out on a celestial journey. Through dark forests and treacherous mountains, they climbed higher and higher, until they reached the heavens themselves.

Finally, standing before the Sun and the Moon, Kofi spoke with a voice filled with sincerity, "Dear Sun and Moon, your light brings us joy and wonder. Your unity is essential for the harmony of our world. Please, come back and shine upon our land."

Moved by Kofi's heartfelt plea, the Sun and the Moon embraced, their rays intertwining in a beautiful dance of warmth and luminescence. They realized that their true strength lay not in separation but in unity.

From that day forward, the Sun and the Moon found their home in the vast sky, casting their light upon the Earth. And the people rejoiced, for they had witnessed the power of togetherness and the beauty that lies in celebrating differences.

<u>Lessons</u>

*The tale of "Why the Sun and the Moon Live in the Sky" reminds us all of the importance of unity and cooperation.

*It teaches us that even in times of disagreement, coming together with love and understanding can create a brighter and more harmonious world.

MWINDO THE BRAVEST WARRIOR (CONGO)

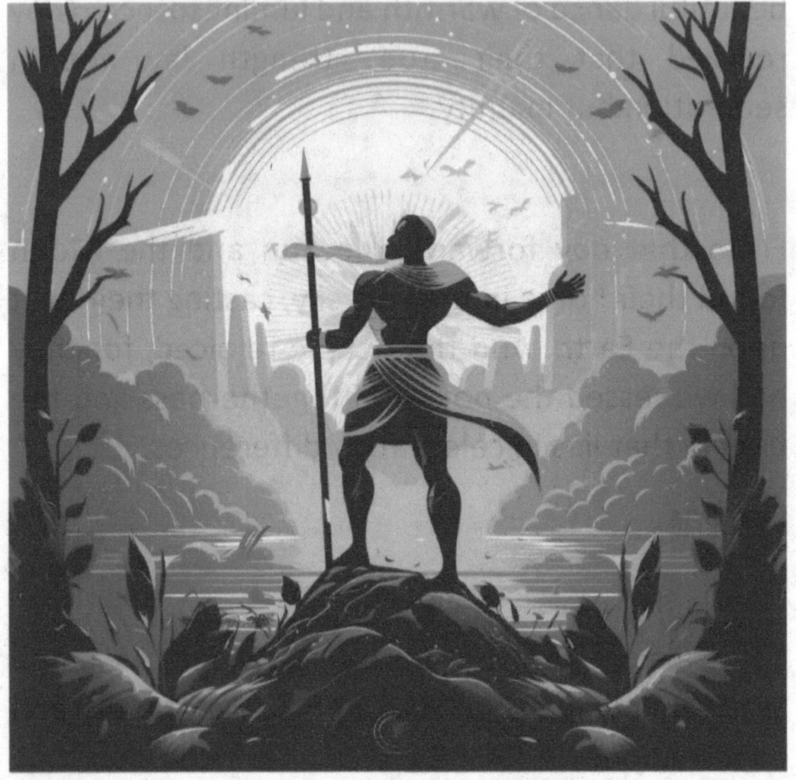

Once upon a time, in the heart of the Congo rainforest, there lived a young and brave warrior named Mwindo. He was no ordinary warrior, for he possessed incredible strength and magical powers. Mwindo was born to bring peace and prosperity to his people, the Bantu tribe, and his story has been passed down through generations.

As a child, Mwindo displayed extraordinary talents. He could speak to animals, summon powerful spirits, and control the elements with a mere flick of his wrist. His father, Nkuba, recognized Mwindo's special gifts and knew that his destiny was far greater than anyone could imagine.

One day, an evil sorceress named Nyanga grew envious of Mwindo's powers and sought to eliminate him. She feared that his strength and goodness would overshadow her dark magic. Determined to stop him, Nyanga placed a curse on Mwindo, causing him to be born prematurely and abandoned in a forest.

But destiny had other plans for Mwindo. The forest animals, who recognized his extraordinary potential, took him in and raised him as their own. They nurtured him, teaching him their ways and guiding him through the challenges of the forest.

As Mwindo grew older, he embarked on a quest to discover his true identity and fulfill his purpose. With his loyal animal companions by his side, he ventured into treacherous lands, battling fearsome creatures and facing incredible trials. Along his journey, he encountered wise elders, benevolent spirits, and mischievous tricksters, each providing him with valuable lessons and magical gifts.

Mwindo's courage and determination captured the attention of his people, who had long awaited their destined leader. They rejoiced as he returned, ready to liberate them from the clutches of oppression and restore harmony to their land.

With the help of his newfound allies, Mwindo confronted the wicked Nyanga, using his extraordinary powers and wisdom to overcome her dark spells. He demonstrated that love, compassion, and bravery were far stronger than any sorcery.

Mwindo's triumph not only secured the safety of his people but also served as a powerful symbol of hope and resilience. His story became a legend, inspiring generations of children to embrace their unique gifts and stand up against injustice.

Lessons

* This story teaches us to embrace our own extraordinary powers, believe in ourselves, and let our light shine bright.

*Just like Mwindo, you have the strength within you to make a difference in the world and stand up in the face of injustice.

THE SACRED DRUM (SENEGAL)

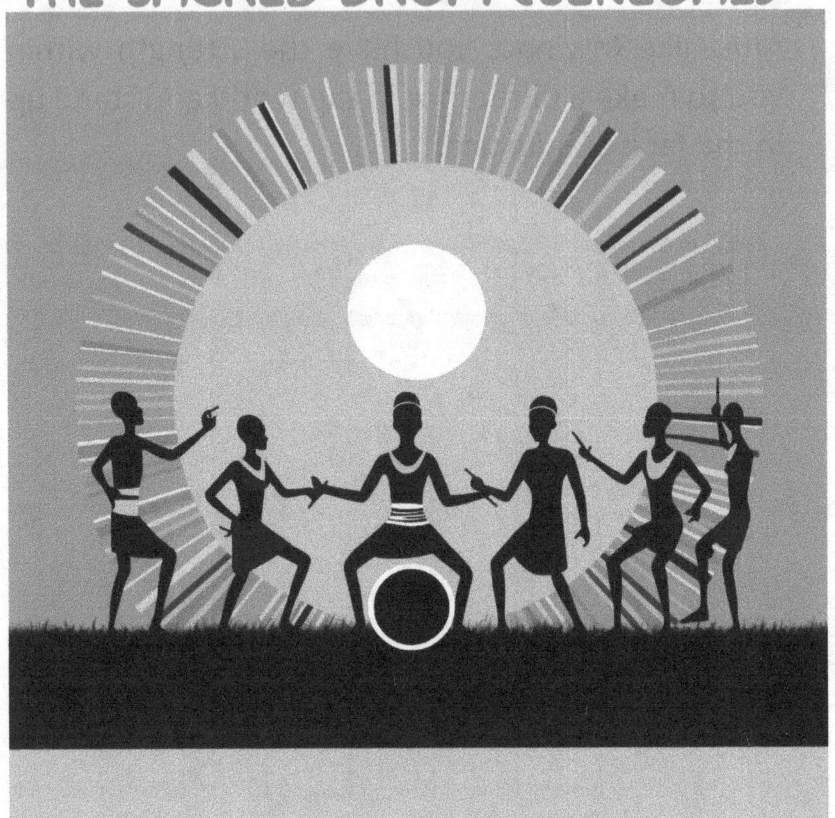

Once upon a time, in the enchanting land of Senegal, there was a village nestled amidst lush greenery and golden savannahs. The villagers believed in the power of storytelling and the magic of their ancient traditions. But there was one treasure that held the hearts of the people more than anything else – the Sacred Drum.

This drum was not just any ordinary instrument. It was said to be a gift from the spirits, blessed with mystical powers. Crafted from the mighty baobab tree, its surface was adorned with intricate carvings depicting the animals of the wild — elephants, lions, and graceful gazelles.

The Sacred Drum had been a part of the village for generations, passing down its legendary tale from elders to children. It was believed that when played with skill and reverence, the drum had the power to summon the spirits, communicate with nature, and even heal the sick.

The story went that long ago, a young boy named Samba, with a heart full of curiosity and a soul filled with rhythm, stumbled upon the Sacred Drum hidden deep within a secret cave. As he touched its weathered surface, a surge of energy coursed through him, connecting him to the spirits of his ancestors.

Samba soon discovered that the drum had a voice of its own. It whispered ancient melodies, carrying the essence of the village's past. He would spend hours in the shade of the baobab tree, listening to the drum's stories, and learning the rhythms that echoed through the ages.

Word of Samba's connection with the Sacred Drum spread throughout the village, and the people flocked to witness this extraordinary bond. They marveled as Samba's fingers danced across the drum's surface, creating music that touched their souls and transported them to distant lands.

But with great power came great responsibility. Samba realized that the drum must be protected and respected, for it held the secrets of their heritage and the wisdom of their ancestors. He became the guardian of the Sacred Drum, vowing to pass down its legacy to future generations.

Every year, during the full moon festival, the village would gather around a bonfire, their eyes sparkling with anticipation. Samba would step forward, the Sacred Drum in his hands, and the air would become charged with excitement. As he played, the rhythm wrapped around the hearts of the villagers, uniting them in a joyous celebration of their African heritage.

<u>Lessons</u>

*The legend of the Sacred Drum in Senegal reminds us of their rich culture and the importance of embracing their roots.

*The drum beats is a constant reminder of the benefits of unity, strength, and the enduring power of tradition.

THE HEROIC LEOPARD WOMAN (CAMEROON)

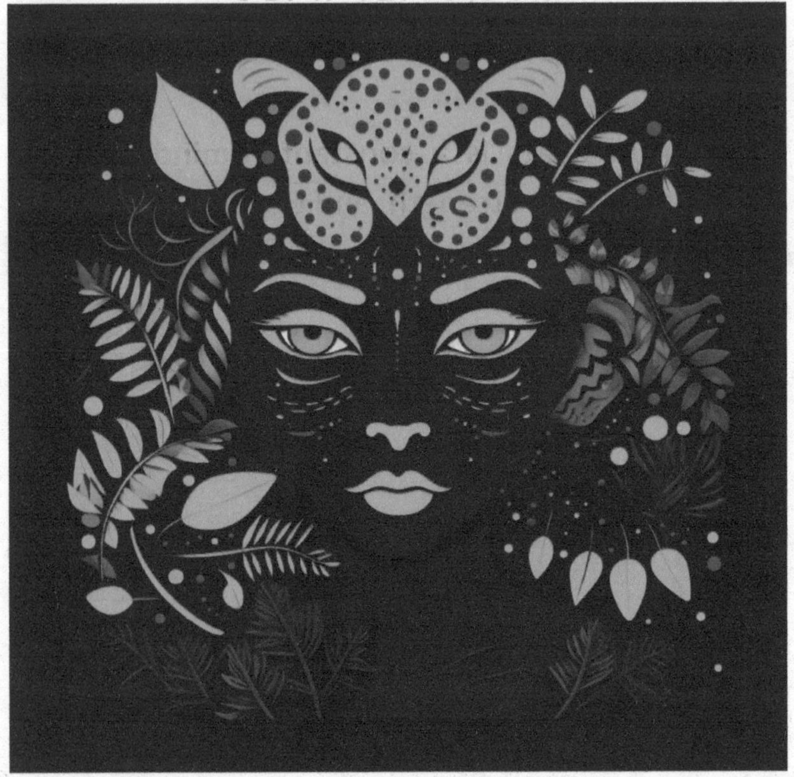

Once upon a time, in the lush and mysterious land of Cameroon, there lived a woman unlike any other. She was known as the Leopard Woman, and her legend echoed through the ancient forests and vibrant villages. This captivating tale takes us on a thrilling journey into the heart of African folklore.

In the depths of the dense jungle, the Leopard Woman roamed gracefully, her coat adorned with mesmerizing spots that shimmered like stars in the night sky. Her eyes gleamed with a mix of cunning and wisdom, as if she held secrets that only the forest could fathom. The villagers whispered tales of her mysterious powers and the enigmatic connection she shared with the wild.

Long ago, when the world was still young, the Leopard Woman had been a human, but her love for the forest was so strong that she yearned to become part of its untamed beauty. One night, under the soft glow of the moon, she made a solemn promise to the spirits of the forest. In return for her devotion, they transformed her into a leopard, forever uniting her destiny with the untamed wilderness.

With each step, the Leopard Woman prowled through the jungle, protecting the creatures that called it home. She danced with the wind, her every movement a testament to grace and power. The animals revered her presence, for she held the wisdom of the ages within her soul.

But there came a time when a great danger threatened the forest. A group of hunters, driven by greed and ignorance, sought to capture the majestic leopard and claim her as a trophy. News of their wicked plan reached the Leopard Woman's ears, and her heart filled with sorrow and determination.

Summoning all her courage, she devised a plan to outsmart the hunters. With her unparalleled speed and agility, she led them on a wild chase through the labyrinthine paths of the jungle. She bounded effortlessly from branch to branch, her spots blending with the dappled sunlight filtering through the canopy.

The hunters grew weary and disoriented, their steps heavy with exhaustion. But the Leopard Woman never faltered. She finally led them to the edge of a mighty waterfall, where they stood in awe of its breathtaking beauty. Seizing the opportunity, she vanished into the foliage, leaving the hunters empty-handed and humbled by nature's power.

From that day forward, the Leopard Woman became a legend, a symbol of strength and wisdom. Her tale spread far and wide, reminding all who heard it of the importance of protecting the natural world and embracing its wonders.

So, my young friends, as you embark on your own adventures, remember the story of the Leopard Woman. Let her inspire you to be guardians of the earth, to tread lightly upon its soil, and to celebrate the extraordinary bond between humans and the magnificent creatures that share our planet.

In the heart of Africa, where legends come alive, the spirit of the Leopard Woman roams free, reminding us all of the enchanting power of our African heritage.

<u>Lessons</u>

* The significance of the Leopard Woman's story symbolizes the harmony between humans and nature, teaching us to respect and cherish the delicate balance that exists in our world.

*Through her tale, children can learn the importance of coexistence and the deep connection between all living beings.

THE STORY OF NYAMI NYAMI THE SERPENT GOD (ZAMBEZI RIVER. ZIMBABWE)

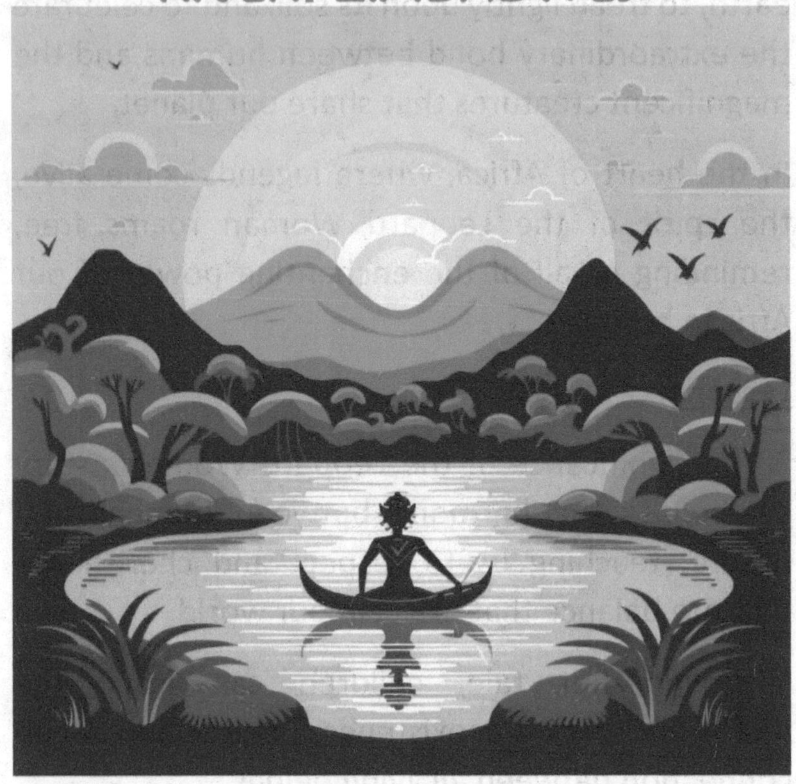

Once upon a time, deep within the heart of Africa, there flowed a mighty river known as the Zambezi. This great river was home to a remarkable creature named Nyami Nyami, a legendary and powerful serpent-like deity.

In the land surrounding the Zambezi, people cherished the river and depended on its waters for their livelihood. They believed that Nyami Nyami was the guardian and protector of the river, watching over them and ensuring their well-being. Nyami Nyami was not just a creature; it was a symbol of unity, strength, and harmony.

According to the ancient tales passed down through generations, Nyami Nyami had a body as long as the river itself, with shiny scales that glistened in the sunlight. Its eyes sparkled with wisdom, and its presence brought a sense of peace to those who believed.

The story of Nyami Nyami begins with a time of great drought that plagued the land. The people suffered, their crops withered, and the animals grew weak. Desperate for relief, they prayed to Nyami Nyami, their faithful protector.

One day, as the sun kissed the horizon, a terrible storm gathered in the distance. Thunder roared, and lightning danced across the sky. The people's hearts filled with hope as they believed Nyami Nyami had heard their prayers.

But then disaster struck. A colossal flood swept across the land, devastating everything in its path.

The people were filled with fear and confusion, for they had never witnessed such a catastrophe. They wondered why Nyami Nyami, their beloved guardian, had unleashed such destruction.

As the floodwaters receded, the people discovered that Nyami Nyami's mate, who had been separated from it, had caused the flood out of loneliness and longing. Nyami Nyami, being a creature of love and loyalty, had unleashed its fury to reunite with its beloved partner.

Realizing the depth of Nyami Nyami's devotion, the people felt remorse for doubting their protector. They understood that the flood was a symbol of love and sacrifice. From that day forward, the people vowed to honor and respect Nyami Nyami and the power of the Zambezi River.

To this day, the story of Nyami Nyami remains significant in the lives of the people living near the Zambezi River. So, my dear young friends, whenever you see a mighty river flowing or hear the rumble of thunder, remember the story of Nyami Nyami. Just like Nyami Nyami, may you always find strength and unity in the powerful currents of your own heritage.

Lessons

*Embrace the lessons it teaches about love, loyalty, unity and the incredible force of nature.

*This reminds us of the incredible force of nature and the importance of cherishing it.

THE LEGEND OF BULU (BETI, CAMEROON)

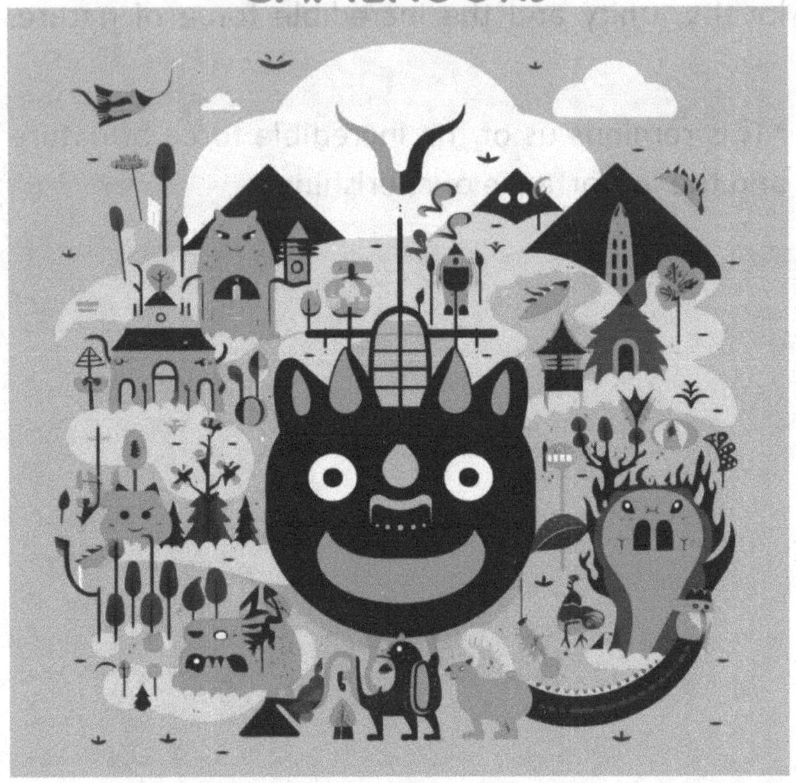

Once upon a time, in a faraway village nestled deep in the lush rainforest of Cameroon, there lived a courageous young girl named Bulu. She had a heart full of curiosity and a spirit as bright as the golden sun. Bulu was adored by all, not only for her kindness but also for her love for adventure.

The Beti people, who called this village home, believed in the power of nature and the spirits that dwelled within it. Amongst them was a legendary creature known as the Mbom, a mysterious and majestic being with the body of a lion and the wings of an eagle. It was said that the Mbom protected the villagers and brought them good fortune.

One fateful day, as the sun cast its warm glow over the village, a darkness fell upon the land. The Mbom had mysteriously disappeared, leaving the villagers in despair. Crops withered, rivers dried up, and the once-thriving village began to fade.

Bulu, with her unwavering courage and determination, could not bear to see her people suffer. She embarked on a brave journey through the dense jungle, guided only by the whispers of the wind and the rustling of leaves. Her heart beat with anticipation as she ventured deeper into the unknown.

As she trekked through the enchanted forest, Bulu encountered many obstacles. She encountered treacherous swamps, where crocodiles lurked beneath the murky waters. She braved dense thickets, where thorny vines tangled and twisted. She even faced the piercing eyes of venomous snakes, slithering silently through the undergrowth.

But Bulu remained undeterred. Her spirit burned brightly, igniting a path of hope. Her determination propelled her forward until, at last, she reached a hidden clearing. Before her stood a majestic waterfall, cascading with a thunderous roar. And there, atop a moss-covered rock, sat the mighty Mbom, its wings tucked gently by its side.

With her heart pounding, Bulu approached the magnificent creature and spoke with utmost respect, pouring her genuine concern for her village into her words. The Mbom listened intently, its wise eyes gleaming with understanding. It explained that it had grown weary, and the village needed to prove their love and appreciation for the natural world.

Inspired by the Mbom's wisdom, Bulu returned to her village and shared the message. The villagers united in their efforts to restore harmony with nature. They planted seeds, tended to the land, and danced under the moonlight, celebrating the gift of life.

Months passed, and gradually, the village began to flourish once more. Lush greenery spread across the landscape, and the rivers flowed with crystal-clear water. The Mbom, touched by the villagers' determination, returned to its rightful place, soaring high above the village, its wings outstretched.

Lessons

*The Legend of Bulu taught us the importance of respecting and nurturing the natural world.

THE DANCING IJELE MASQUERADE (ANAMBRA, NIGERIA)

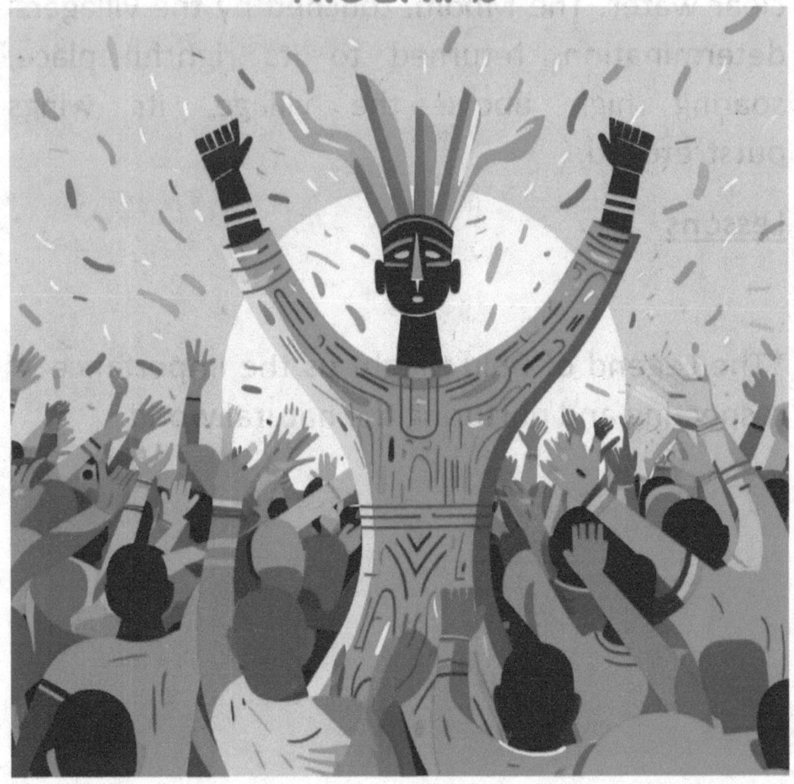

Once upon a time, in the beautiful land of Anambra, Nigeria, there was a captivating folktale that captured the hearts and imagination of the people. It was the enchanting story of "The Dancing Ijele Masquerade."

Long ago, the people of Anambra celebrated a grand festival every year. They called it the Ijele Festival, and it was a time when the entire community came together to honor their ancestors and celebrate their rich cultural heritage. At the heart of this joyous occasion was the legendary Dancing Ijele Masquerade.

Legend has it that the Ijele Masquerade was the largest and most magnificent of all the masquerades in Anambra. It stood tall and proud, adorned with colorful feathers, dazzling beads, and shimmering masks. The rhythmic beat of drums echoed through the air as the Ijele Masquerade gracefully moved through the village streets, captivating everyone who laid eyes upon it.

Now, let me take you back in time to discover the history of this remarkable tradition. Many generations ago, a wise and courageous ancestor named Nso-ani had a dream. In his dream, the spirits of the forest appeared to him, revealing the secrets of the Ijele Masquerade. They told Nso-ani that the Ijele represented the connection between the earthly realm and the spiritual realm. It was a symbol of unity, strength, and respect for the ancestors.

Inspired by this divine revelation, Nso-ani shared his vision with the village elders. They were amazed by his story and recognized the importance of preserving their cultural heritage. Together, they decided to bring the Ijele Masquerade to life. Skilled craftsmen spent months crafting the most splendid costume, ensuring that every detail reflected the grandeur and significance of the masquerade.

As the years went by, the Ijele Masquerade became a symbol of pride and identity for the people of Anambra. It symbolized their rich history, their strong community bond, and their deep respect for their ancestors. During the Ijele Festival, children and adults would eagerly gather to witness the mesmerizing dance of the masquerade. Its graceful movements, synchronized with the rhythm of the drums, seemed to transport everyone into a world of magic and wonder.

So, dear young readers, the story of "The Dancing Ijele Masquerade" holds a special place in the hearts of the people of Anambra, Nigeria. It is a tale that weaves together history, culture, and a sense of belonging. As you listen to the rhythmic beat of the drums and watch the graceful movements of the masquerade, remember to cherish your own heritage, celebrate your traditions, and embrace the stories that make you who you are.

Lessons

*The significance of the Ijele Masquerade serves as a reminder to the young ones about the importance of their African heritage.

*It teaches unity, respect, and the power of storytelling.

THE SPIRIT OF THE BAOBAB TREE (ZARIA, NORTHERN NIGERIA)

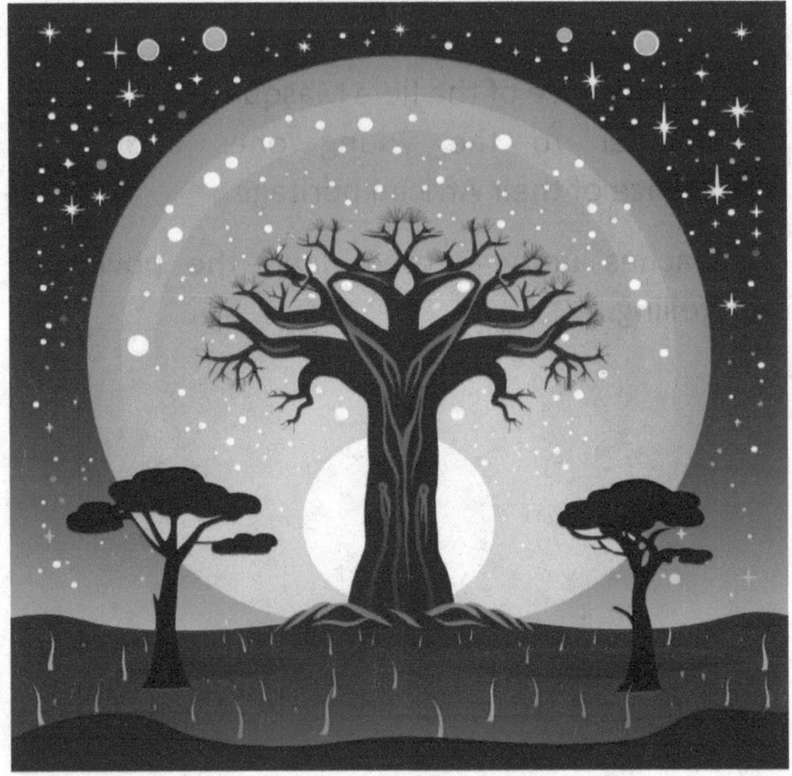

Once upon a time, in the beautiful land of Zaria, nestled in Northern Nigeria, there stood a majestic baobab tree. This towering wonder of nature was no ordinary tree. It was said to be the dwelling place of a mysterious and enchanting spirit known as Asara.

Legend has it that long ago, when the world was still young, the baobab tree possessed great powers. Its ancient roots stretched deep into the earth, connecting it to the heart of the land. Its branches reached high into the sky, whispering secrets to the clouds. The baobab tree was a silent witness to the stories of time, the secrets of the animals, and the dreams of the people.

The tale of the Spirit of the Baobab Tree spread far and wide because of the magical occurrences that took place beneath its protective branches. The people believed that Asara, the spirit within, was responsible for these wondrous happenings.

Children would gather around the baobab tree, listening eagerly as their elders shared tales of Asara's benevolence. It was said that when the rains failed to fall, Asara would summon the rain gods with her melodious songs, and the parched land would be nourished once again. The farmers relied on her to bless their crops, ensuring an abundant harvest each year.

But that wasn't all. Asara was known to be a protector of the animals, too. When a lost or injured creature sought refuge near the baobab tree, the spirit would provide healing and shelter, nursing them back to health.

The Spirit of the Baobab Tree was a symbol of wisdom and strength. Asara was said to have lived for centuries, observing the rise and fall of kingdoms, the changing seasons, and the harmony of nature. People believed that if they listened carefully, the baobab tree would whisper ancient wisdom into their ears.

So, my young friends, the next time you see a magnificent baobab tree standing tall, take a moment to appreciate its beauty and think about the wondrous tales it holds. Close your eyes and imagine the gentle whispers of Asara, the Spirit of the Baobab Tree, carrying the hopes and dreams of generations past.

And remember, just like the baobab tree, you too possess incredible strength and wisdom within you. Embrace your heritage, listen to the stories of your ancestors, and let your imagination soar as high as the branches of the baobab tree.

For in these tales lie the magic of Africa, waiting to be discovered by curious hearts like yours.

<u>**Lessons**</u>

*The significance of this folktale lies in its connection to African heritage. It symbolizes resilience, community, and the wisdom of the ancestors.

*The tale of the Spirit of the Baobab Tree reminds us of our deep connection to the natural world and the importance of nurturing and protecting it.

THE LEGEND OF PRINCESS MALIKA (HAUSA. NIGERIA)

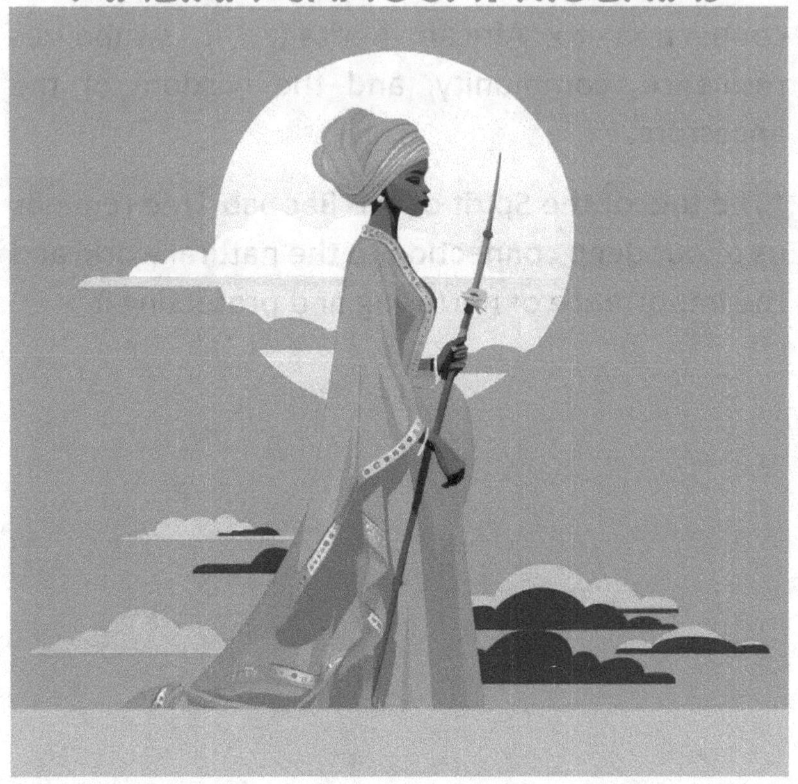

Once upon a time, in the ancient land of Hausa, there lived a courageous princess named Malika. She was known far and wide for her bravery, kindness, and unwavering spirit. But have you ever wondered how this legendary tale came to be?

Many moons ago, the people of Hausa faced great challenges. A fearsome dragon named Abari wreaked havoc on their villages, causing destruction and spreading fear among the people. The land was desperate for a hero to save them from this terrifying creature.

In the heart of Hausa, nestled amidst the towering hills and golden plains, stood the grand palace of the wise King Bello. He was a fair and just ruler who cared deeply for his people. One night, as King Bello gazed at the stars, he had a vision. He dreamt of a brave and fierce princess who would rise above all odds to defeat the mighty dragon.

The next morning, King Bello called upon his subjects and shared his prophetic vision. The people were filled with hope, for they believed that this brave princess could bring peace and prosperity to their land. And so, the legend of Malika began to spread like wildfire, capturing the imagination of everyone who heard it.

Malika, a young girl with a heart full of determination, lived in a humble village near the palace. She had always dreamt of embarking on great adventures and making a difference in the world. When she heard of the king's vision, a fire ignited within her. Malika knew that she was the one destined to face the dragon and protect her people.

With unwavering courage, Malika set out on her journey to find the dragon's lair. She traveled through dense forests, crossed treacherous rivers, and climbed towering mountains. Along the way, she encountered wise old sages who shared their knowledge and bestowed upon her magical gifts.

As Malika approached the dragon's lair, she could feel her heart pounding with excitement and fear. She knew that her people were counting on her, and she could not let them down. With her newfound allies and the power of her magic, she confronted Abari, the fearsome dragon.

A mighty battle ensued between Malika and the dragon, shaking the earth and filling the sky with fiery sparks. Malika fought with all her might, using her wits, bravery, and the lessons she had learned from the sages. It was a battle of epic proportions, but in the end, Malika emerged victorious, banishing the dragon from the land of Hausa forever.

News of Malika's triumph spread throughout the kingdom like wildfire. The people rejoiced, celebrating their brave princess who had saved them from destruction. Malika's tale became an integral part of Hausa's history, passed down from generation to generation.

So, my dear young readers, as you hear the legend of Malika, let it ignite a fire within your hearts. Remember that you too can be a hero, facing your own dragons and making a positive impact on the world around you.

<u>Lessons</u>

*The legend of Malika continues to inspire young boys and girls, reminding them of the power of courage, determination, and standing up for what is right.

*It teaches us that no matter how big the challenges may seem, we all have the strength within us to overcome them.

THE TALKING SKULL (NIGERIA)

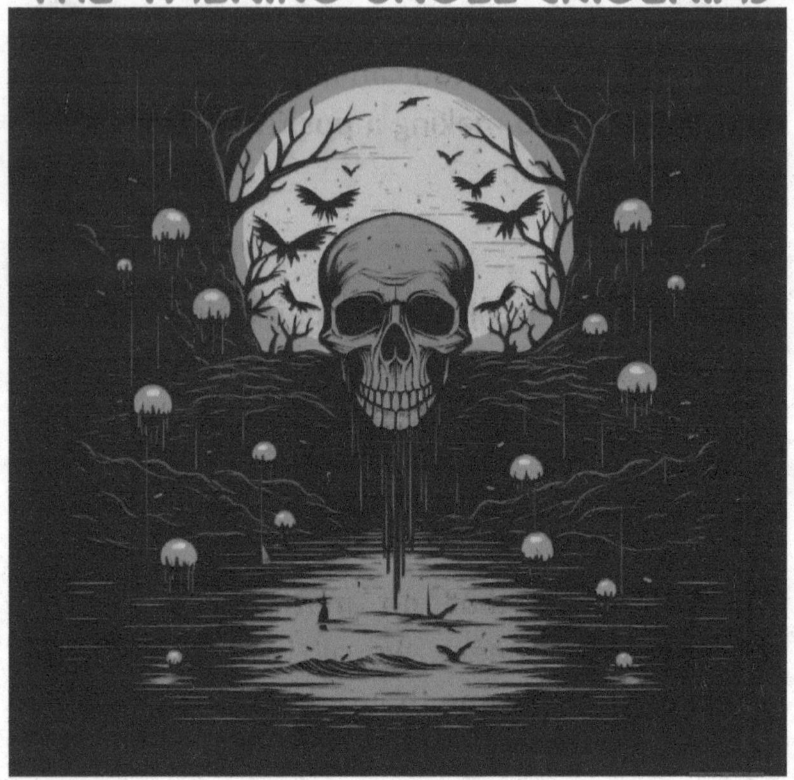

Long ago, in a small village nestled amidst lush green hills and flowing rivers, there lived a man named Mabo. Mabo was known for his silver tongue, always eager to share tales and gossip with anyone who would lend an ear. His words traveled faster than the wind, as he couldn't resist the temptation to talk about everything he saw or heard.

One fateful day, while exploring the mysterious depths of the dense forest, Mabo stumbled upon a peculiar sight. Beneath a gnarled old tree, half-buried in the earth, lay a gleaming skull, its hollow sockets seemingly staring at him. To his astonishment, as he approached, the skull began to speak!

"Who dares disturb my eternal slumber?" the skull boomed, its voice echoing through the ancient trees. Mabo's eyes widened in disbelief, for he had never encountered anything so extraordinary. Excitement bubbled within him, and he couldn't wait to share this marvelous discovery with the world.

With great enthusiasm, Mabo rushed back to the village, unable to contain his excitement. He told everyone he met about the talking skull, regaling them with tales of its magical powers and wise words. But alas, the villagers, skeptical and wary, dismissed Mabo's claims as mere fabrication.

Word of Mabo's extraordinary encounter quickly spread across the land. People from far and wide came to see the talking skull for themselves, hoping to witness this marvel with their own eyes. But every time they gathered, the skull remained silent, refusing to speak on cue. Doubt began to seep into their hearts, and they accused Mabo of weaving a web of lies.

As mistrust grew, a sinister plot was hatched by the jealous villagers. They conspired to teach Mabo a lesson, for they believed he had deceived them all. Under the cover of darkness, they led Mabo deep into the heart of the forest, where danger lurked in every shadow.

Unaware of the impending danger, Mabo stood amidst the towering trees, his heart pounding with anticipation. Suddenly, a figure emerged from the darkness, a menacing expression etched upon their face. It was the village chief, adorned in traditional garb, ready to pass judgment on Mabo for his alleged deception.

But just as the chief raised his hand to strike, a low, haunting voice pierced the silence. "Stop!" commanded the talking skull, its words filled with ancient wisdom and truth. The villagers froze in fear, realizing the skull's power and authenticity.

With the truth finally revealed, Mabo was spared from harm. The villagers, now humbled and repentant, recognized the significance of the talking skull. They learned the importance of discerning truth from falsehood and the consequences of spreading tales without caution.

And so, the tale of "The Talking Skull" became deeply ingrained in the hearts and minds of the Cameroonian people. It served as a reminder to honor the power of words, to speak truthfully, and to weigh our words before they are unleashed into the world.

Lessons

*This tale teaches one to listen carefully, think critically, and consider the consequences of their words.

*To learn the value of truth, the importance of discernment, and the richness of African traditions.

THE GODDESS MAMI WATA (EFIK, SOUTH EAST NIGERIA)

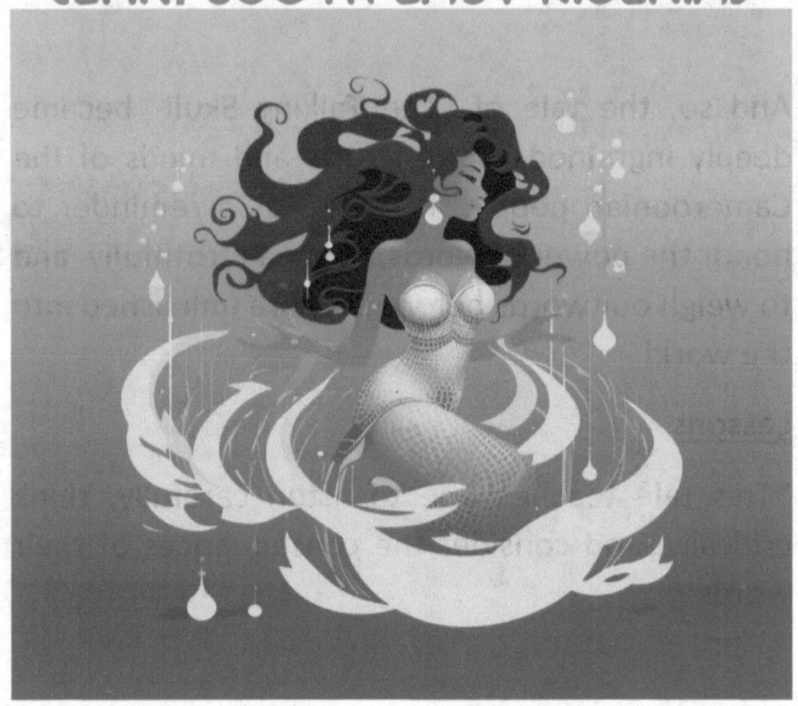

Once upon a time, in the lush and vibrant lands of Southeast Nigeria, there lived a legendary goddess known as Mami Wata. Her name means "Mother Water," for she ruled over the sparkling rivers and mysterious depths of the ocean. Let me take you on a wondrous journey to discover the captivating tale of the Goddess Mami Wata and uncover the secrets of her enchanting realm.

Long ago, the Efik people, who dwelled by the shores of the Cross River, shared stories of a beautiful and majestic deity who possessed the power to control the waters. Mami Wata was said to have the body of a woman, adorned with iridescent scales that shimmered like the colors of the rainbow. Her long, flowing hair cascaded like waves, and her voice echoed with the melody of a thousand singing birds.

Legends spoke of Mami Wata's ability to grant blessings of wealth, fertility, and protection to those who honored her. She would emerge from the depths, riding on the backs of dolphins and surrounded by fish of every hue. With a graceful flick of her tail, she could calm turbulent waters and ensure a bountiful harvest for the fishermen.

But Mami Wata's tales weren't just about her beauty and benevolence. The Efik people believed that she possessed a mischievous and sometimes tempestuous nature. She could be both generous and demanding, rewarding her followers with good fortune or teaching them lessons through challenges.

The history of the folktale of Mami Wata's origin is as intriguing as the goddess herself. It is said that when African communities were forcefully taken away during the transatlantic slave trade, their traditions traveled with them across the ocean. Mami Wata became an enduring symbol of African heritage, blending with other cultures and evolving over time. Today, she is revered not only in Nigeria but in various parts of Africa and the African diaspora.

The popularity of Mami Wata's story lies in its magical allure and its reflection of the deep connection between humans and water. Water, in African culture, is regarded as a source of life, cleansing, and spiritual power. Mami Wata embodies these aspects, capturing the imagination of children and adults alike, inspiring awe and wonder.

<u>Lessons</u>

*The tale of the Goddess Mami teaches us to respect and cherish the waters that sustain us, reminding us of our responsibility to protect the environment.

*Mami Wata symbolizes the strength, beauty, and divine power that can be found within every individual, encouraging us to embrace our own unique qualities.

THE LEGEND OF LEBOMBO (ZULU, SOUTH AFRICA)

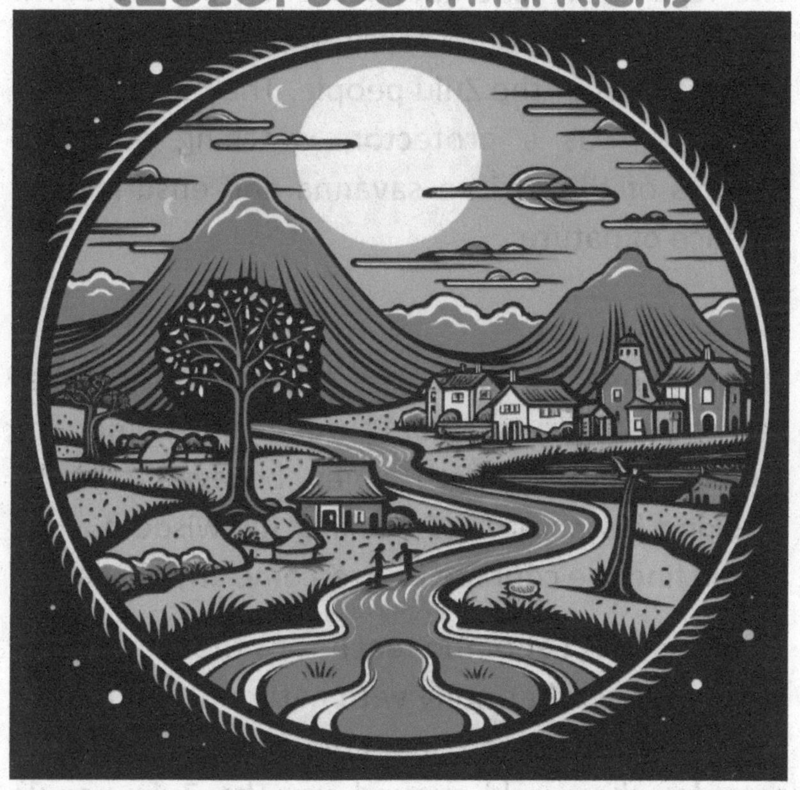

Once upon a time, in the vast plains of South Africa, there was a legendary creature named Lebombo. Lebombo was no ordinary creature; he possessed the strength of a lion, the wisdom of an elephant, and the speed of a cheetah. With his magnificent, golden mane and sparkling eyes, he roamed the land, spreading awe and wonder wherever he went.

The legend of Lebombo has been passed down through generations, capturing the hearts and imaginations of the Zulu people. They believe that Lebombo was a protector, watching over the animals of the African savanna and ensuring the balance of nature.

Many moons ago, when the Zulu tribe faced great hardships, their ancestors turned to Lebombo for guidance and strength. They believed that by invoking his name and seeking his wisdom, they would find the courage to overcome any challenge.

The legend of Lebombo teaches us the importance of respect and harmony with nature. It reminds us that we are all interconnected and that we must care for the world around us. The Zulu people celebrate Lebombo's legacy through storytelling, dance, and music during special ceremonies.

Now, let me share with you a thrilling tale that has been whispered among the Zulu children for ages:

In the heart of the African savanna, a young boy named Mbali embarked on an extraordinary adventure. One sunny morning, as he wandered near the great Lebombo Mountain, he discovered an ancient cave hidden amidst the tall grasses.

Curiosity got the better of Mbali, and he cautiously stepped into the dark abyss. Inside, he found himself surrounded by vivid paintings, telling the story of Lebombo's heroic deeds and his powerful spirit.

As Mbali marveled at the magnificent artwork, he felt a gentle breeze sweep through the cave. Suddenly, a voice echoed in his ears, "Young one, you have shown great curiosity and respect for our traditions. I shall grant you a gift."

In disbelief, Mbali looked around but saw no one. Yet, he couldn't ignore the whispering wind that seemed to guide him further into the cave. As he walked deeper, the paintings became more vibrant, and the legend of Lebombo unfolded before his eyes.

Mbali learned about the times when Lebombo protected the animals from poachers, how he healed the sick and injured, and how he danced under the moonlight, bringing joy to the Zulu people.

With each step, Mbali felt a surge of courage and determination flowing through his veins. He knew that he had been chosen to carry the legacy of Lebombo forward.

As Mbali emerged from the cave, he noticed a change in himself. His eyes sparkled like Lebombo's, and he felt a newfound strength within. From that day on, Mbali dedicated his life to protecting the environment, just as Lebombo had done before him.

Lessons

*The legend of Lebombo reminds us to cherish the land, respect the animals, and honor our African heritage.

*It serves as a beacon of hope and inspiration for all those who seek to make a difference in the world.

THE FLYING TORTOISE (SOUTHEASTERN. NIGERIA)

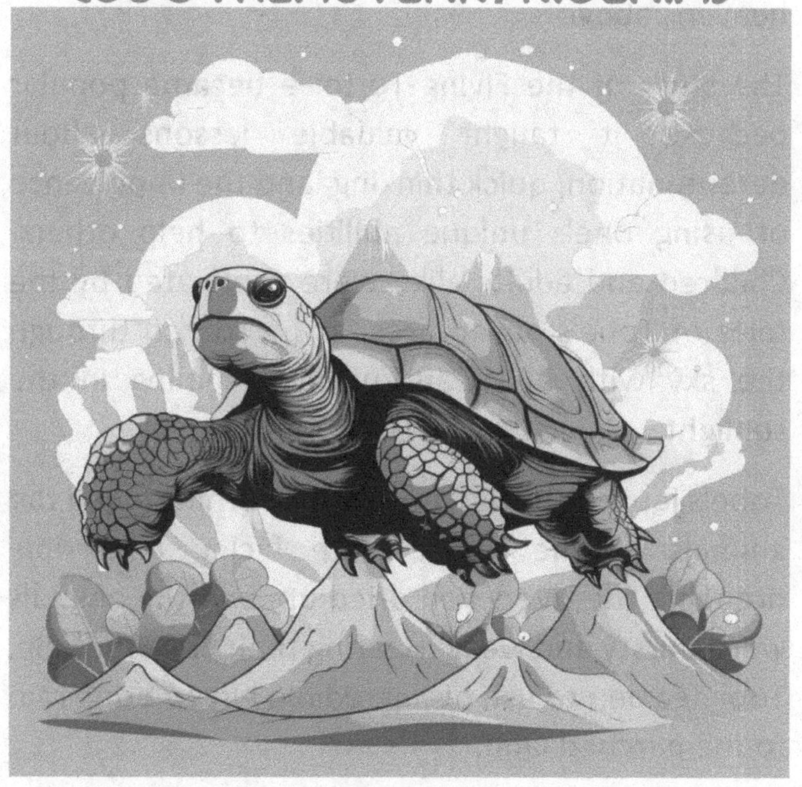

Once upon a time, in the rich green forests of southeastern Nigeria, there lived a clever little tortoise named Tobe. Tobe was not like any other tortoise. He had a special gift that made him truly unique – he could fly!

Legend has it that long ago, when animals and humans lived together in harmony, Tobe's ancestors were granted this incredible ability by the great deity, Obasi. They were chosen to be messengers between the earthly realm and the heavens above.

The story of the Flying Tortoise became popular because it taught valuable lessons about determination, quick thinking, and the importance of using one's unique abilities to help others. Children and adults alike were captivated by the tales of Tobe's adventures, as he soared through the sky with his beautiful shell shining in the sunlight.

Tobe's journey began one sunny morning when the animals of the forest were facing a terrible drought. The rivers had dried up, and the animals were thirsty and weak. Hearing their cries for help, Tobi decided to use his incredible gift to bring rain to the parched land.

With a determined look on his face, Tobe flapped his wings and soared high above the treetops. As he flew, he spotted a mighty eagle perched on a tall tree. With his quick wit, Tobe hatched a plan to persuade the eagle to help him.

Approaching the eagle with a friendly smile, Tobe explained his mission. The eagle was impressed by Tobe's bravery and agreed to carry him even higher into the sky, where they could find the Rain God's dwelling.

Together, they reached the Rain God's palace, which was adorned with vibrant rainbows and sparkling waterfalls. Tobe, with his unwavering determination, pleaded with the Rain God to send rain to the thirsty forest.

The Rain God, moved by Tobe's sincere request, opened the gates of the heavens. Rain poured down in torrents, quenching the land's thirst and bringing life back to the forest. The animals rejoiced, dancing and celebrating under the cool droplets of water.

News of Tobe's extraordinary adventure spread like wildfire, and he became a beloved figure in folklore. Children admired his courage and cleverness, while adults appreciated the underlying message of unity and the power of using one's unique gifts for the greater good.

From that day on, the Flying Tortoise, with his shimmering shell, became a symbol of hope and resilience, reminding everyone that even the smallest among us can achieve great things.

So, dear children, whenever you see a tortoise slowly crawling along, remember the incredible story of Tobe, the Flying Tortoise. Look up at the sky and let your imagination take flight, for within each of us lies the potential for extraordinary adventures.

And just maybe, if you listen carefully, you might hear the faint flapping of wings and catch a glimpse of Tobi soaring through the clouds, continuing his marvelous journey through the ages.

Lessons

*The tale of the flying tortoise teaches that there is power and unity in using your gift for greater good.

*The tale of the flying tortoise is a symbol of hope and resilience.

THE LION AND THE HARE (NIGERIA)

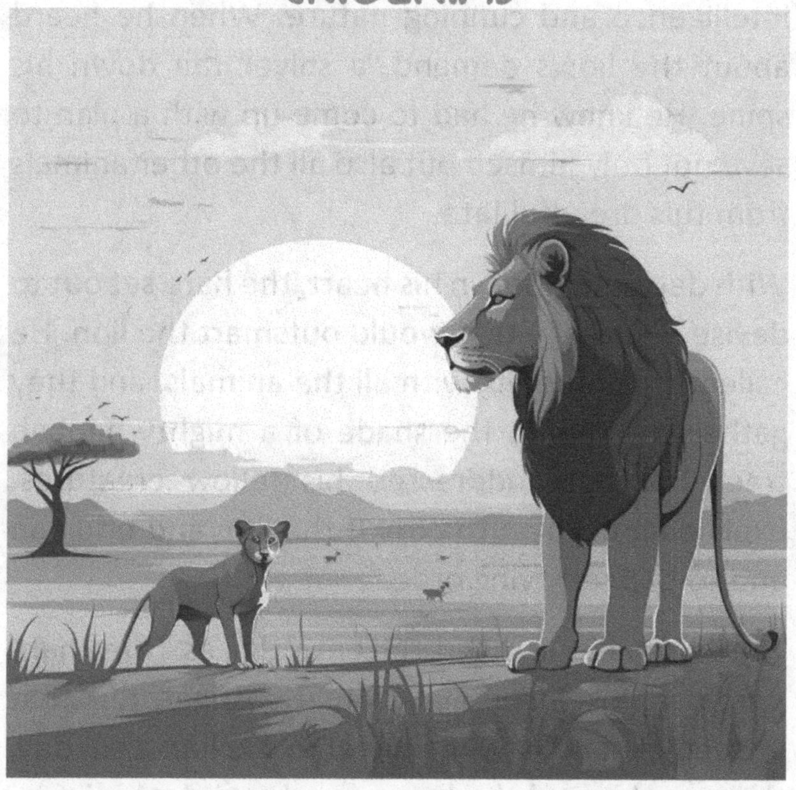

Once upon a time, in the vast grasslands of Nigeria, a group of animals found themselves facing a great challenge. A mighty lion, with a ferocious appetite, had declared that he would devour one animal from the grasslands every single day. Fear spread among the animals, for they knew that it was only a matter of time before the lion's hunger turned towards them.

Among the animals, there lived a clever and quick-witted hare. This hare was known for his intelligence and cunning nature. When he heard about the lion's demand, a shiver ran down his spine. He knew he had to come up with a plan to save not only himself but also all the other animals from this dreadful fate.

With determination in his heart, the hare set out to devise a strategy that would outsmart the lion. He called for a meeting with all the animals, and they gathered beneath the shade of a mighty baobab tree. The hare addressed his fellow creatures, explaining his plan to outwit the lion and bring an end to this terrifying ordeal.

The animals listened attentively as the hare unfolded his ingenious plan. He suggested that instead of sending one animal to the lion each day, they would send the lion a meal so extraordinary, so captivating, that it would satisfy his hunger and keep him entertained for a long time. The other animals were intrigued by this idea, their hope rekindled.

The hare explained that he would be the one to approach the lion, armed with his wit and agility.

He would challenge the lion to a race across the grasslands, promising the lion that if he won, the lion could feast on him. The hare knew he could outrun the lion, for his speed was unmatched.

News of the hare's daring plan spread like wildfire throughout the grasslands. Animals from far and wide gathered to witness this extraordinary race. The lion, always hungry for excitement, accepted the challenge with a roar of anticipation. The stage was set, and the animals waited with bated breath.

As the race began, the hare sprinted like the wind, his little legs carrying him swiftly across the grasslands. The lion, with all his strength, thundered behind the nimble hare. The grasses swayed in their wake as the animals watched in awe.

But the clever hare had a trick up his sleeve. He had marked the racecourse with strategically placed obstacles—a winding path through thorny bushes, a narrow bridge over a rushing river, and a dense forest with twisting trails. The lion, despite his size and power, struggled to maneuver through the obstacles, slowing him down significantly.

With each passing moment, the hare's lead widened, until he was a mere speck on the horizon, leaving the lion far behind. The other animals watched in astonishment as the hare crossed the finish line, victorious and unscathed.

The lion, humbled by the hare's cunning and speed, acknowledged his defeat with a nod of respect. From that day forward, the lion vowed to spare the animals of the grasslands and seek his meals elsewhere. The hare had saved them all from the jaws of the ferocious lion, becoming a hero and a symbol of wit and resourcefulness.

<u>Lessons</u>

*This folktale of "The Lion and the Hare" teaches children the importance of quick thinking, strategy, and the power of wit in overcoming challenges.

*It reminds us that even the smallest and seemingly weakest among us can achieve remarkable feats when armed with intelligence and courage.

THE STORY OF ABUK (DINKA, SOUTH SUDAN)

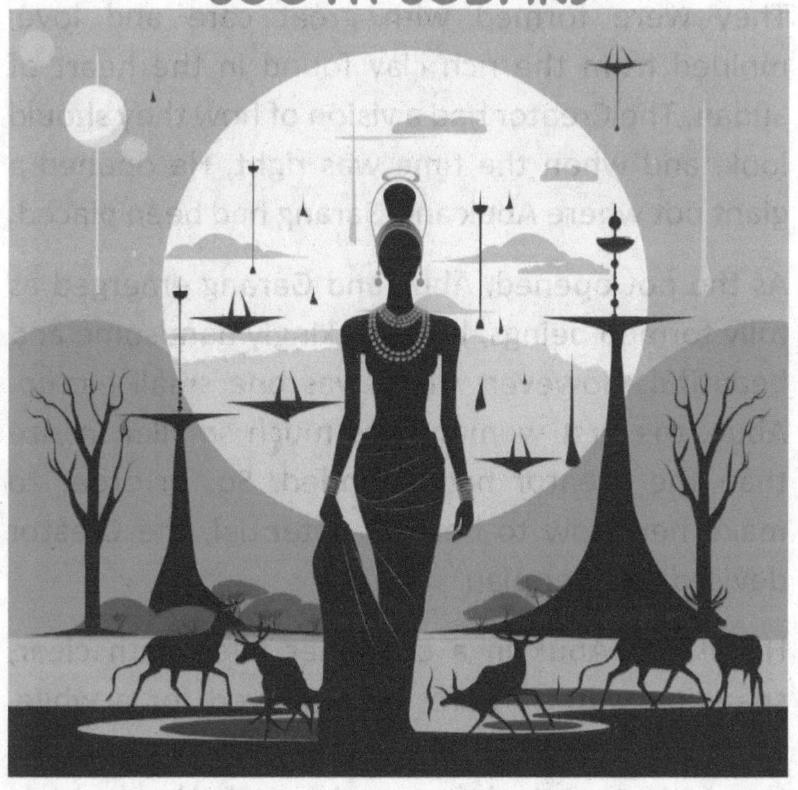

Once upon a time, in the vast and beautiful land of Sudan, there lived a woman named Abuk. She was no ordinary woman, for she held a special place in the hearts of the Dinka people, who believed she was the very first woman in the world. Abuk's story is an ancient folktale passed down through generations, and it is as fascinating as it is significant.

According to the Dinka tradition, Abuk was created by the Creator alongside Garang, the first man. They were formed with great care and love, molded from the rich clay found in the heart of Sudan. The Creator had a vision of how they should look, and when the time was right, He opened a giant pot where Abuk and Garang had been placed.

As the pot opened, Abuk and Garang emerged as fully formed beings, breathtakingly handsome and beautiful. However, there was one small hiccup. Abuk, the first woman, was much smaller in size than the Creator had intended. So, in order to make her grow to her full potential, the Creator devised a clever plan.

He placed Abuk in a container filled with clear, sparkling water. There, Abuk stayed for a while, absorbing the water like a sponge. Day after day, the water worked its magic, and Abuk's body gradually swelled until she reached the size of a regular human being. The Creator was delighted with what he saw.

Life in this world, however, wasn't always easy for Abuk and Garang. They were given just one grain a day for their sustenance, and hunger always lingered within them. But Abuk was a woman of extraordinary intelligence and resourcefulness.

She knew that in order to survive, they had to make the most of what they had.

With her sharp mind and cleverness, Abuk devised a brilliant idea. She transformed the single grain into a nourishing paste, stretching its value to last longer. She also made a decision that would change their lives forever. Abuk saved one grain on alternate days, accumulating them until she had enough to plant and grow her own grain.

Her hard work and dedication bore fruit, quite literally. Abuk's planting of grain became the source of abundance for all. Fields of golden crops flourished, ensuring that no one in the land would go hungry again. The people rejoiced, grateful for Abuk's wisdom and the gift she had shared with them.

And so, the tale of Abuk, the first woman, spread across the land, gaining popularity and significance. It became a cherished part of the Dinka heritage, symbolizing the power of intelligence, resourcefulness, and the importance of sharing one's knowledge with others.

Lessons

*A strong moral of this tale to always remember the strength and resilience that lies within you.

*Just like Abuk, you possess the ability to overcome challenges, find creative solutions, and make a positive impact in the world around you.

THE MAGIC POT (YORUBA, NIGERIA)

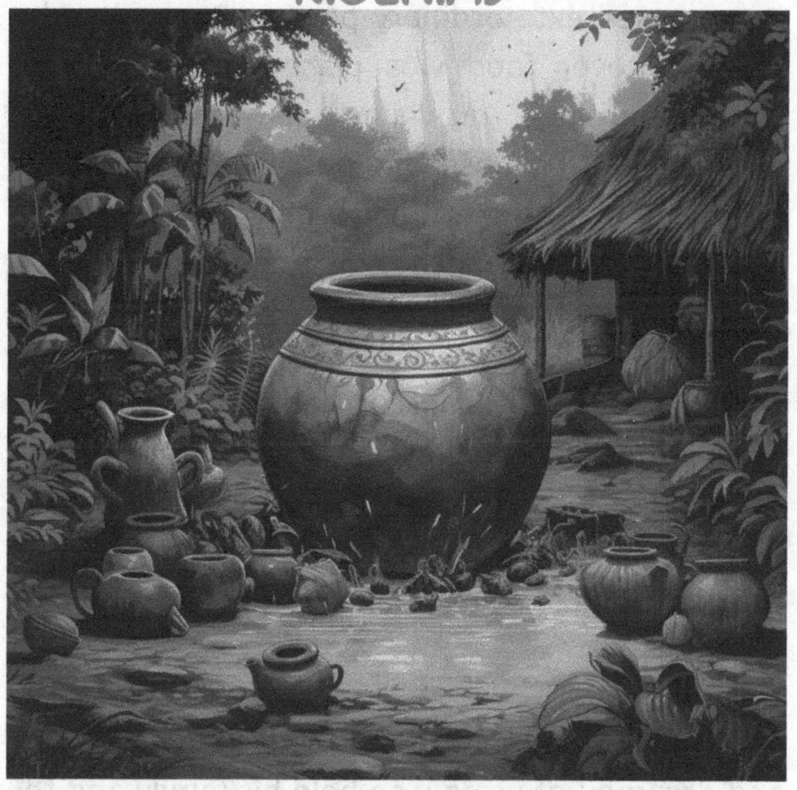

Once upon a time, in a small village nestled deep within the lush forests of Nigeria, there lived a kind-hearted young boy named Ade. Ade's village was known for its rich traditions and enchanting folklore, and one such tale that had been passed down from generation to generation was the story of "The Magic Pot."

The Magic Pot was no ordinary cooking pot. It had been crafted by the ancient gods themselves, and it possessed extraordinary powers. Legend had it that whatever food was placed inside the pot would multiply, providing an abundance of nourishment for those who possessed it. But there was a catch, for the pot had a mind of its own and could only be used by those with pure hearts.

The tale of The Magic Pot had become popular among the villagers, who marveled at the thought of endless food. It was said that the pot had saved many families during times of drought and famine, bringing hope and sustenance to the hungry.

Now, young Ade had heard of this legendary pot and dreamed of using it to help his family and the entire village. His mother, Mama Zara, worked tirelessly to put food on their table, but it was never enough. Ade knew that if he could get his hands on The Magic Pot, he could bring joy and abundance to their lives.

Driven by his pure heart and a desire to make a difference, Ade set off on a journey to find The Magic Pot. His adventure took him through dense forests and across roaring rivers until he reached a hidden cave, where the pot was said to be guarded by a mischievous spirit.

As Ade cautiously entered the cave, he felt a cold breeze brush against his face, and his heart raced with anticipation. Suddenly, he found himself face-to-face with the spirit of the cave. The spirit, impressed by Ade's bravery and noble intentions, decided to test him.

"I will grant you access to The Magic Pot," the spirit said, "but only if you promise to use its powers wisely and share the abundance with those in need."

Ade eagerly agreed, understanding the importance of generosity and gratitude. With the spirit's guidance, he found the pot hidden within the depths of the cave. Its surface shimmered with a magical glow, filling him with awe and wonder.

From that day forward, Ade used The Magic Pot to provide for his family and the villagers. He carefully measured the food they needed and watched in amazement as it multiplied before their eyes. No longer did anyone in the village go to bed hungry, and a sense of joy and unity spread throughout the community.

However, as time went on, Ade noticed a change within himself. The once humble and kind-hearted boy had become consumed by greed. He began to use The Magic Pot excessively, hoarding food for himself and neglecting to share with others.

Soon, the village was gripped by a wave of discontent. The people grew resentful of Ade's selfishness, and a dark cloud of mistrust hung over the once-thriving community. It was then that Ade realized the profound lesson The Magic Pot had been trying to teach him all along—how greed can cause troubles in life.

Filled with regret and a desire to make amends, Ade made a heartfelt apology to his family and the villagers. He promised to mend his ways and restore the harmony that had once prevailed.

With renewed determination, Ade used The Magic Pot to distribute food equitably, ensuring that every family received their fair share. Slowly but surely, trust was rebuilt, and the village once again flourished with unity and compassion.

Lessons

*This tale reminds children of the importance of gratitude, selflessness, and the perils of greed.

*It serves as a reminder that true abundance comes not from possessing material wealth but from sharing and caring for one another.

THE ORPHAN'S TRIUMPH (ZIMBABWE)

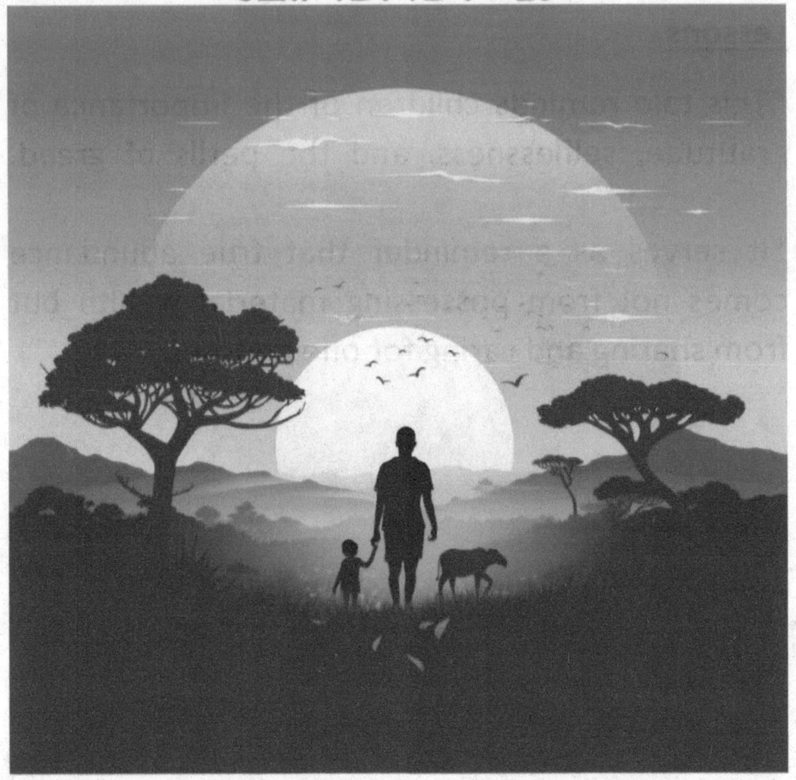

Once upon a time, in the beautiful land of Zimbabwe, there lived a brave and clever young girl named Nyasha. Nyasha was no ordinary girl; she was an orphan, and she had faced many hardships in her life. But despite her difficult circumstances, Nyasha possessed a heart full of resilience and a spirit that shone brightly.

The folktale of "The Orphan's Triumph" has been passed down through generations in Zimbabwe, captivating both young and old. It is a story of hope, determination, and the power of kindness.

Long ago, during a time of great drought, the people of a small village suffered tremendously. Crops withered, rivers ran dry, and the animals grew weak. Nyasha, with her deep love for her community, could not bear to see her fellow villagers suffer. She knew she had to do something.

One day, as Nyasha was wandering through the vast African savannah, she encountered a wise old elephant. The elephant, known as Moyo, sensed the young girl's pure heart and decided to help her. Moyo revealed a secret: hidden deep within the heart of a nearby mountain was a magical lake that held the power to bring rain and restore life to the land.

With newfound hope, Nyasha embarked on a courageous journey to find the enchanted lake. Along her path, she encountered various obstacles, from treacherous terrains to cunning animals. But Nyasha's unwavering determination and cleverness guided her through each challenge.

During her quest, Nyasha also discovered the importance of kindness and compassion. She rescued a trapped lion cub, offered shelter to a lost bird, and shared her meager food with a hungry antelope. Little did she know that these acts of kindness would later play a significant role in her triumph.

Finally, after facing numerous trials, Nyasha reached the heart of the mountain. There, she found the magical lake shimmering with its extraordinary power. With the guidance of Moyo, Nyasha called upon the spirits of the land, asking for rain to save her village and its people.

As the rain poured down from the heavens, the drought-stricken land began to transform. The crops flourished, the rivers flowed once more, and life returned to its vibrant state. Nyasha's village rejoiced, and her fellow villagers hailed her as a true hero.

"The Orphan's Triumph" is a cherished folktale in Zimbabwe because it represents the enduring spirit and resilience of the people. It teaches us that even in the face of adversity, we can find strength within ourselves and make a positive impact on the world around us.

This remarkable tale reminds us of the importance of kindness, empathy, and the interconnectedness of all living beings. Nyasha's acts of compassion not only helped her on her journey but also saved her village, showing us the profound significance of extending a helping hand to others.

<u>Lessons</u>

*This is a tale reminding you to embrace the values of courage, kindness, and determination as you navigate through life.

*Just like Nyasha, you too have the power to make a difference and create a better world for all.

THE STORY OF KINTU (BUGANDA, UGANDA)

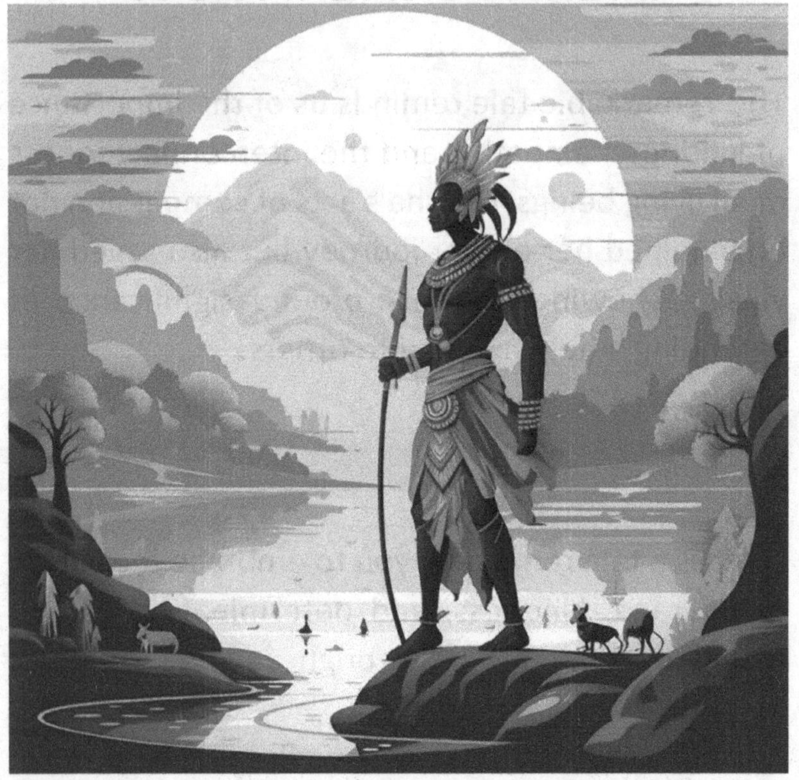

Once upon a time, in the vast land of Buganda, Uganda, there existed a captivating folktale known as "The Story of Kintu." Gather around, young ones, as I weave a tale of wonder and magic, passing down the treasured heritage of our African ancestors.

In the distant past, long before our time, Kintu was the only person on earth. Imagine, dear children, a world with just one soul, accompanied only by his faithful companion—a gentle cow that provided him with milk and company. Oh, how Kintu longed for someone to share his joys and sorrows!

Meanwhile, high up in the heavens, a wise and mighty being named Ggulu reigned over all creation. Ggulu had many children, each with their unique gifts and powers. But there was one thing missing in Ggulu's divine realm—the presence of humans on earth.

Filled with compassion and love, Ggulu decided to grant Kintu's deepest wish. He summoned his children and declared, "My dear ones, it is time to bring life and companionship to Kintu. Descend to earth and let the bond of humanity begin."

With great excitement, the heavenly children descended, guided by the warm glow of the sun. Each child possessed a special gift, bestowed upon them by Ggulu. Some were blessed with great strength, others with remarkable wisdom, and still others with extraordinary talents.

One by one, the heavenly children met Kintu, and their encounters were nothing short of miraculous. They formed deep friendships, creating a community where laughter echoed through the valleys and love blossomed in every heart. Kintu was no longer alone, for he had found his family.

But as with any tale of wonder, challenges arose. Envious of the happiness on earth, Walumbe, a dark and mischievous spirit, sought to disrupt the harmony. Walumbe spread illness and discord, threatening to tear the newfound community apart.

Yet, our courageous heroes did not falter. Kintu and his celestial companions, armed with their unique gifts, confronted Walumbe and vowed to protect their cherished bond. Their unity and determination prevailed, banishing Walumbe's darkness and restoring peace to their beloved land.

And so, dear children, the story of Kintu became a beacon of hope and resilience for generations to come. It is a tale of how friendship and unity can overcome even the greatest challenges, reminding us that we are never truly alone.

"The Story of Kintu" holds great significance in Buganda and throughout Uganda. It is not merely a tale but a reflection of our rich history and the enduring spirit of our people. This story has been passed down from generation to generation, reminding us of our roots, our strength, and our interconnectedness with the world around us.

Lessons

*This folklore emphasizes the importance of friendship, unity, and the power of compassion. *It should inspire you to cherish the bonds you form, just as Kintu and his heavenly companions cherished theirs.

THE CLEVER HARE (SOUTHWESTERN. MADAGASCAR)

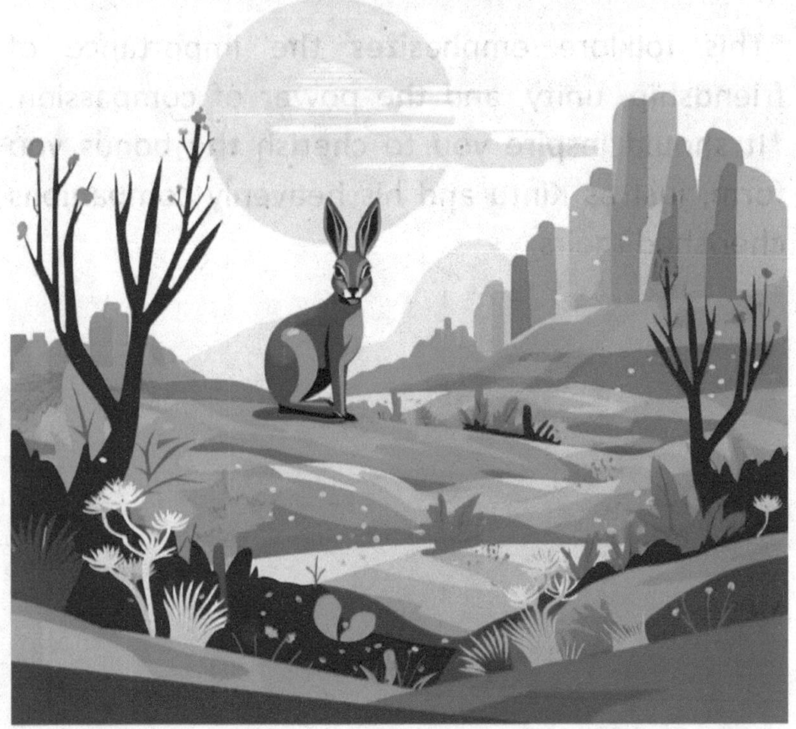

Once upon a time, in the breathtaking landscapes of southwestern Madagascar, there lived a clever little hare named Rano. Rano was known throughout the forest for his wit, quick thinking, and mischievous ways. He had long ears that could pick up even the faintest sound and a fluffy white tail that he would twitch whenever he had a cunning plan brewing.

Now, let me tell you how the thrilling folktale of "The Clever Hare" came to be and why it is cherished by the people of Madagascar. Generations ago, the people of this land discovered the extraordinary intelligence of the hare through their encounters with the mischievous yet cunning Rano. They were fascinated by his ability to outsmart even the trickiest of situations, and they shared his adventures with great enthusiasm.

This tale became popular as it spread from village to village, passed down from parents to children, and became an integral part of the rich oral tradition of the Malagasy people. The story of "The Clever Hare" has not only entertained generations but also taught valuable lessons about the power of wit, resourcefulness, and thinking on one's feet.

In "The Clever Hare and the Mischievous Monkey," Rano finds himself challenged by a mischievous monkey named Matoke. Matoke was notorious for his pranks and loved to cause trouble for the other animals in the forest. One day, Matoke decided to play a trick on Rano by stealing his beloved carrot patch.

But Rano, being the clever hare that he was, knew he couldn't let the thieving monkey get away with it. He devised a plan to outwit Matoke and teach him a lesson he would never forget. With his cunning mind and lightning-fast reflexes, Rano set out to reclaim his carrots and show Matoke the consequences of his mischievous actions.

The tale takes us on a thrilling journey through the lush forest, where Rano encounters a series of obstacles that test his wit and agility. Along the way, he seeks help from his friends, the wise owl and the patient tortoise, who offer him valuable advice and guidance.

Through a series of clever ruses and hilarious encounters, Rano ultimately outsmarts Matoke, teaching him a lesson about the importance of honesty, friendship, and respecting others. The story ends with Rano's carrot patch restored and a newfound understanding between the hare and the monkey.

"The Clever Hare and the Mischievous Monkey" continues to captivate the hearts and minds of children in Madagascar and beyond. It reminds us all that intelligence and resourcefulness can help us overcome challenges, solve problems, and build lasting friendships.

Lessons

*It emphasizes the importance of using your intelligence to overcome challenges and find clever solutions when faced with adversity.

*It showcases the value of quick thinking, creativity, and the ability to outsmart those who underestimate you.

ADANNA THE FIREMAKER'S DAUGHTER (NIGER DELTA, NIGERIA)

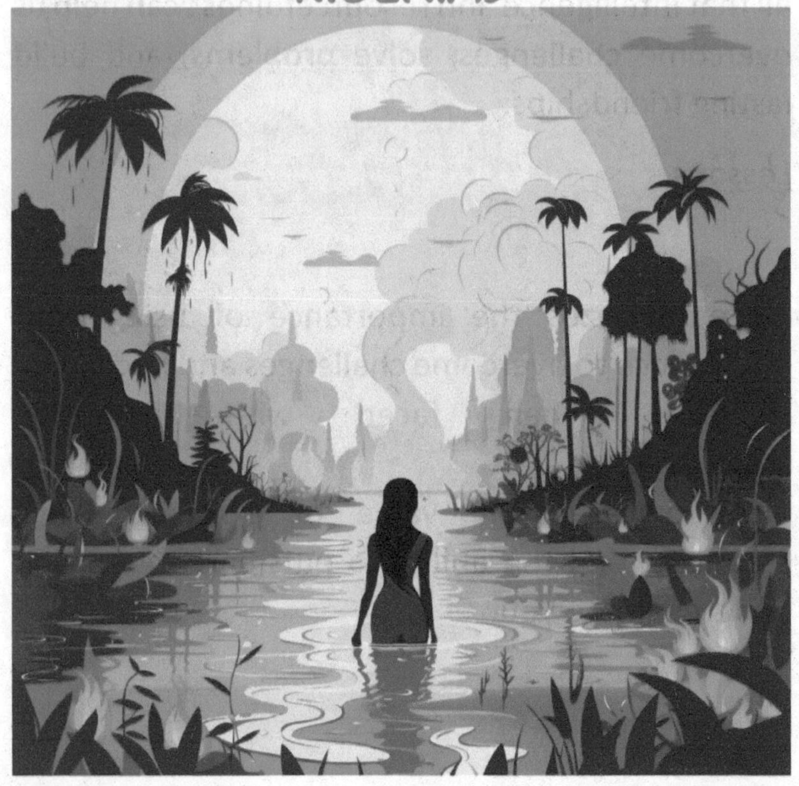

Once upon a time in the ancient land of Nigeria, where stories whispered through the winds and legends danced in the hearts of its people, there lived a young girl named Adanna. She was known far and wide as "The Firemaker's Daughter," for she possessed a remarkable gift that set her apart from others.

Adanna's village, nestled in the lush greenery of the Niger Delta, was filled with laughter and joy. But it was also a place of darkness when the sun would dip below the horizon, leaving the villagers in need of warmth and light. That is when Adanna would step forward, her spirit ignited with determination.

As dusk descended upon the village, Adanna would gather sticks and dry leaves, her nimble hands swiftly working their magic. With a single strike of her stone against the flint, sparks would fly and catch hold of the dry tinder. Flames leaped and crackled, casting a golden glow upon Adanna's face. She had the power to summon fire, a gift passed down through generations.

But how did the tale of "The Firemaker's Daughter" come to be? Well, legend has it that long ago, a mighty fire spirit fell in love with a mortal woman. Together, they had a daughter who inherited the spirit's fiery gift. As the years passed, Adanna's remarkable abilities became known, and her tale began to spread across the land.

The story of "The Firemaker's Daughter" became popular because it symbolized the strength and resilience of the Nigerian people. Fire, in their culture, represented warmth, illumination, and the eternal spark of life. Adanna embodied these qualities and became a beacon of hope for her village, teaching them to embrace their inner light even in the darkest of times.

Lessons

*Fire here symbolizes transformation, courage, and the power to ignite change.

*Adanna's story reminds us that within each of us lies the power to create, to bring warmth and light to our communities, and to inspire others with our unique gifts.

THE LEGEND OF NYAMI NYAMI (KARIBA LAKE. ZIMBABWE)

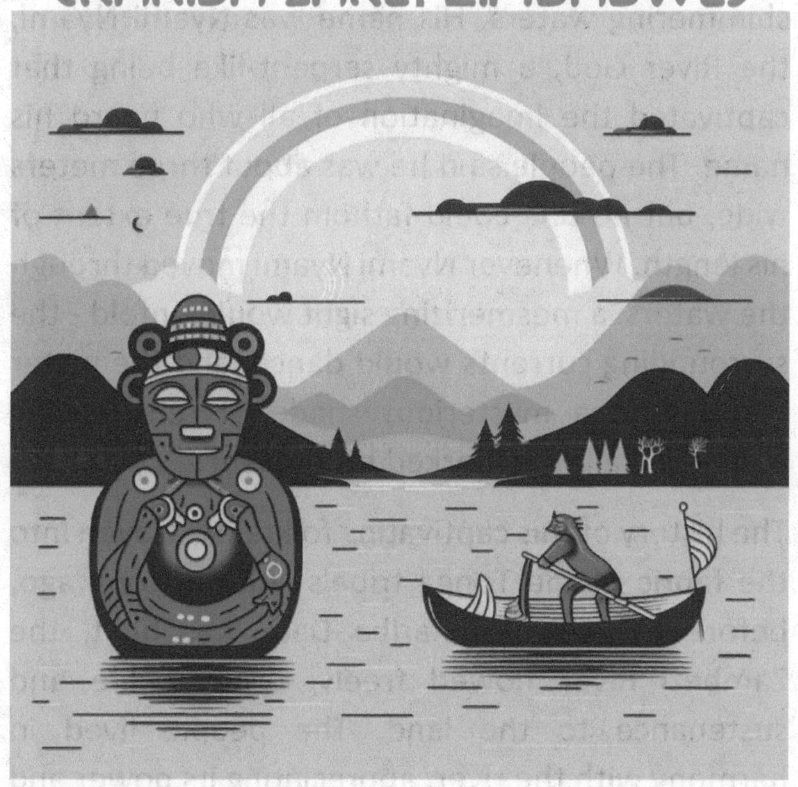

Once upon a time, in the beautiful land of Zimbabwe, nestled within the enchanting Zambezi Valley, there was a majestic lake called Kariba. Surrounding this sparkling lake, the Tonga tribe shared a tale that was passed down through generations, a tale of wonder and mystery known as "The Legend of Nyami Nyami."

In the heart of Kariba Lake, it was believed that an extraordinary creature dwelled beneath the shimmering waters. His name was Nyami Nyami, the River God, a mighty serpent-like being that captivated the imagination of all who heard his name. The people said he was about three meters wide, but no one could fathom the true extent of his length. Whenever Nyami Nyami moved through the waters, a mesmerizing sight would unfold - the surrounding currents would dance, and the water would turn a mysterious shade of red, leaving behind a trail that marked his presence.

The history of this captivating folktale is woven into the fabric of the Tonga tribe's culture. Long ago, before the colossal Kariba Dam was built, the Zambezi River flowed freely, bringing life and sustenance to the land. The people lived in harmony with the river, appreciating its power and blessings. But when the dam was constructed, the river's flow was disrupted, and the tranquil world the Tonga people knew was forever changed.

As the waters rose, separating the land and forming the vast Kariba Lake, a deep sense of loss and longing enveloped the Tonga tribe. They felt a profound connection to the river, and they believed that Nyami Nyami, their guardian deity, had been separated from them. It was during this time of change and upheaval that the legend of Nyami Nyami was born.

Children, imagine standing by the shores of Lake Kariba, the gentle breeze caressing your cheeks as you gaze out over the vast expanse of water. The sun casts a golden glow, and you wonder if Nyami Nyami, the mighty River God, might just emerge from the depths. You envision the waters swirling and turning red as he gracefully moves through his domain, protecting the land and its people.

As you listen to the stories whispered by the elders of the Tonga tribe, you feel a connection to the ancient tales that have been passed down for centuries. The Legend of Nyami Nyami beckons you to explore the wonders of African mythology, to honor the wisdom and traditions of the Tonga people, and to celebrate the awe-inspiring beauty of the natural world.

<u>Lessons</u>

*The tale of Nyami Nyami represents their deep respect for nature's power and the desire to be reunited with their guardian deity.

*The Nyami Nyami is a symbol of hope and resilience, reminding them of the enduring spirit that resided within their hearts.

THE ADVENTURES OF JABU AND SIBO (SWAZILAND)

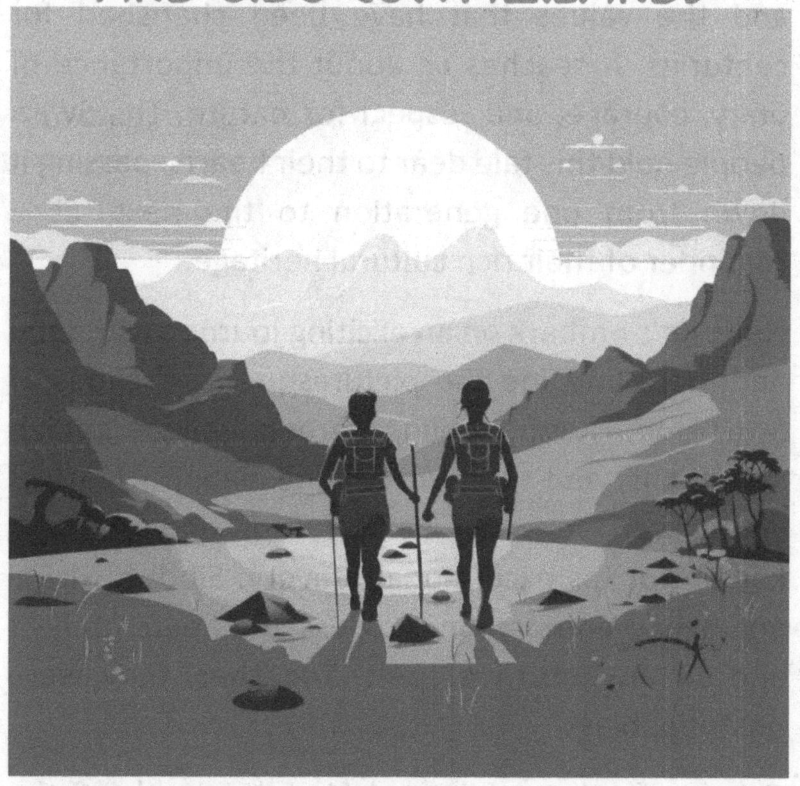

Long ago, in the heart of Swaziland, there was a mystical mountain called Emlembe, which reached high into the sky, almost touching the clouds. Legends whispered that a powerful spirit dwelled within its peaks, granting wisdom and protection to the Swazi people. This tale of bravery and friendship, known as "The Adventures of Jabu and Sibo," was born from the whispers of the wind.

The story of Jabu and Sibo became popular because it captured the essence of Swazi heritage and the values that have been cherished for centuries. It teaches us about the importance of unity, courage, and respect for nature. The Swazi people hold this tale dear to their hearts, passing it down from one generation to the next, as a reminder of their rich cultural heritage.

Now, let's embark on an exciting journey with Jabu and Sibo. Imagine the picturesque landscapes of Swaziland, with rolling green hills, golden savannahs, and majestic wildlife. Jabu, a fearless young warrior with a heart full of kindness, was known for his exceptional bravery. Sibo, his loyal and clever companion, possessed a keen intellect and an adventurous spirit. Together, they were unstoppable!

One fateful day, while exploring the depths of the enchanted forests surrounding Emlembe, Jabu and Sibo stumbled upon an ancient map hidden beneath a moss-covered rock. It revealed a secret treasure that lay deep within the heart of the mountain. Eager to unravel its mysteries, they embarked on a quest that would change their lives forever.

Their journey took them through treacherous terrains, across roaring rivers, and into the heart of a hidden cave. Along the way, they encountered mythical creatures, wise old sages, and magical spirits who tested their courage and rewarded their determination.

As Jabu and Sibo delved deeper into the mountain, they discovered not only the fabled treasure but also a newfound understanding of themselves and their connection to their Swazi heritage. They learned that bravery comes in many forms, and true wealth lies in the bonds of friendship and the preservation of their traditions.

So, my young friends, let your imagination soar high above the clouds of Swaziland as you join Jabu and Sibo on their extraordinary quest. Together, we will celebrate the magic of friendship and the beauty of Swazi traditions that have been passed down from generation to generation.

Remember, the tales of our ancestors hold great wisdom and joy. They connect us to our past and inspire us to shape a bright future. Let the Adventures of Jabu and Sibo be a beacon of light, reminding us of the strength and beauty found within our African heritage.

<u>**Lessons**</u>

*"The Adventures of Jabu and Sibo" symbolizes the spirit of exploration and the power of unity.

*It encourages young Swazi children to embrace their heritage, honor their roots, and always pursue their dreams with bravery and compassion.

THE LEGEND OF TILO (LESOTHO)

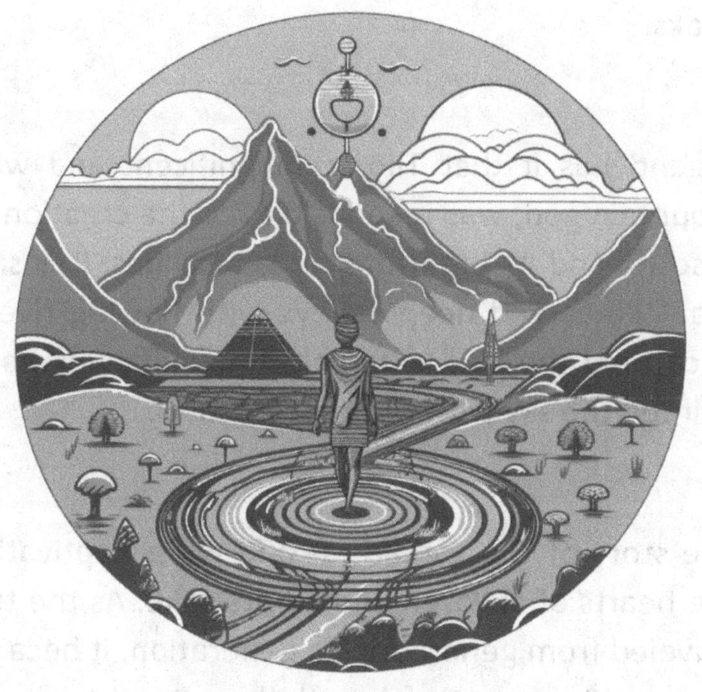

Once upon a time, nestled high in the beautiful mountains of Lesotho, there was a legend that filled the hearts of the people with awe and wonder. It was the legendary tale of Tilo, the Magical Mountain Kingdom.

Long, long ago, before the world was touched by the hands of time, Lesotho was a land blessed by the presence of ancient gods and goddesses. The mighty mountains stood tall, watching over the land like giant protectors, and it was believed that a powerful deity named Tilo resided within their peaks.

Legend has it that Tilo, a magnificent and wise mountain god, was responsible for the creation of Lesotho and its breathtaking landscapes. It is said that Tilo carved deep valleys with flowing rivers, decorated the land with colorful wildflowers, and painted the sky with vibrant rainbows.

The story of Tilo spread far and wide, captivating the hearts of children and adults alike. As the tale traveled from generation to generation, it became an important part of Lesotho's cultural heritage. The people believed that Tilo's spirit inhabited the mountains, blessing their crops with fertile soil, bringing rain during dry spells, and protecting the kingdom from harm.

Children in Lesotho would gather around their elders, eager to hear the enchanting tale of Tilo. They would listen in awe as the elders described the magical dances of the spirits that dwelled among the mountaintops. The elders would paint vivid pictures with their words, describing how the sun would rise, casting a golden glow on the peaks, and how the moon would illuminate the valleys during the night, creating a magical aura.

Remember, dear children, the Legend of Tilo reminds us to cherish the wonders of nature and embrace the stories that connect us to our roots. Let your imagination soar as you embark on this captivating journey through the enchanted kingdom of Tilo, where mountains hold secrets, and legends come to life.

Lessons

*The Legend of Tilo teaches the people to respect and honor nature, for it is believed that Tilo's spirit is intertwined with the land.

*The legend also emphasizes the importance of unity, as the people of Lesotho come together to celebrate and pay homage to the great mountain god during special ceremonies and festivals.

THE HUNTER AND THE ANTELOPE (CAMEROON)

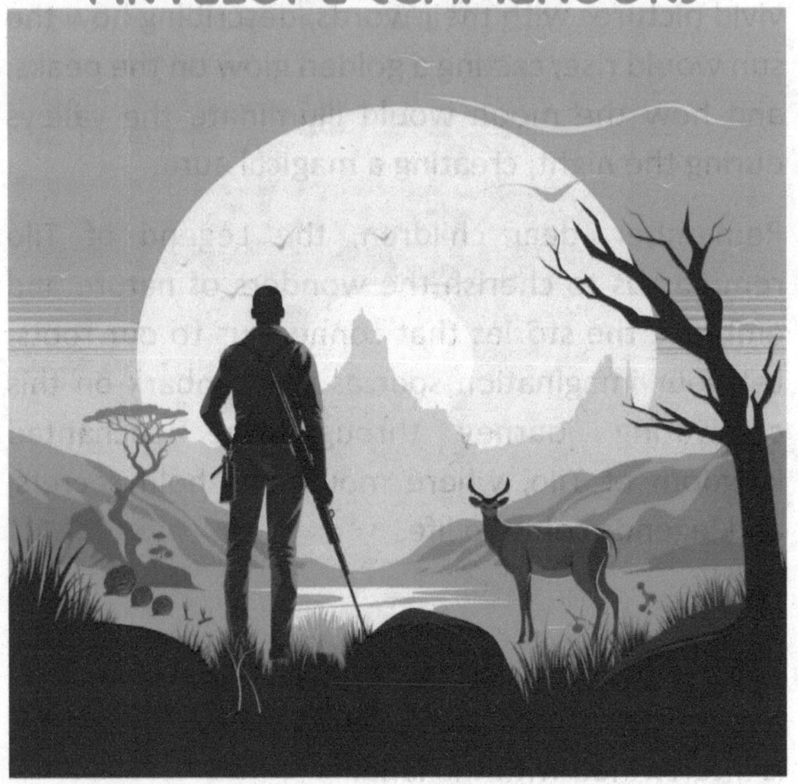

Once upon a time, in the lush forests of Cameroon, lived a skilled hunter named Kofi. Kofi was known far and wide for his bravery and sharp aim with his bow and arrow. He respected the balance of nature and always treated the animals with kindness and gratitude.

One sunny morning, as Kofi was quietly stalking his prey, he stumbled upon a distressed crocodile caught in a trap. The crocodile pleaded for help, promising to reward Kofi if he set it free. Kofi's heart swelled with compassion, and without hesitation, he released the crocodile from its trap.

As the crocodile slithered back into the river, it turned to face Kofi with a mischievous glint in its eye. "Thank you, dear hunter. I shall indeed fulfill my promise," the crocodile hissed, its voice laced with cunning.

Curiosity mixed with caution, Kofi asked, "What reward do you have In mind, honorable crocodile?"

The crocodile's toothy grin widened. "You have shown me great kindness, and for that, I will share with you the wisdom of the animals. Seek the antelope, the owl, the spider, and the tortoise. Each holds a different opinion on what debt of gratitude truly means."

Kofi, intrigued by this mysterious task, embarked on a journey to find these wise creatures. His first stop was the grassy plains where the graceful antelope roamed. The antelope spoke with elegance, explaining that gratitude meant helping others without expecting anything in return. Kofi listened intently, cherishing the antelope's wise words.

Next, Kofi ventured deep into the forest and found the wise old owl perched high in a tree. The owl, with its hooting voice, shared that gratitude meant showing respect and appreciation for the gifts received from others. Kofi nodded, captivated by the owl's wisdom.

The spider, spinning intricate webs in its delicate web, taught Kofi another lesson. Gratitude, said the spider, meant using one's talents to make a positive difference in the world. Kofi marveled at the spider's intricate creations and pondered the importance of using his skills for the greater good.

Finally, Kofi sought the wise tortoise, who resided near a peaceful pond. The tortoise, known for its slow and deliberate nature, explained that gratitude meant repaying kindness by sharing it with others. Kofi nodded in understanding, appreciating the tortoise's gentle wisdom.

Armed with the wisdom of the antelope, the owl, the spider, and the tortoise, Kofi returned to the river, where the crafty crocodile awaited. With newfound clarity, Kofi looked into the crocodile's eyes and spoke firmly, "Gratitude is not a mere token of words. It is a heartfelt understanding, a harmony of actions that create a better world."

The crocodile's jaws dropped in surprise, realizing that Kofi had learned the true essence of gratitude. From that day forward, the crocodile abandoned its devious plans and swore to protect and respect all living creatures.

<u>Lessons</u>

*The story of "The Hunter and the Antelope" shows the importance of gratitude, wisdom, and the interconnectedness of all beings.

THE DEITIES OF DAHOMEY (BENIN. NIGERIA)

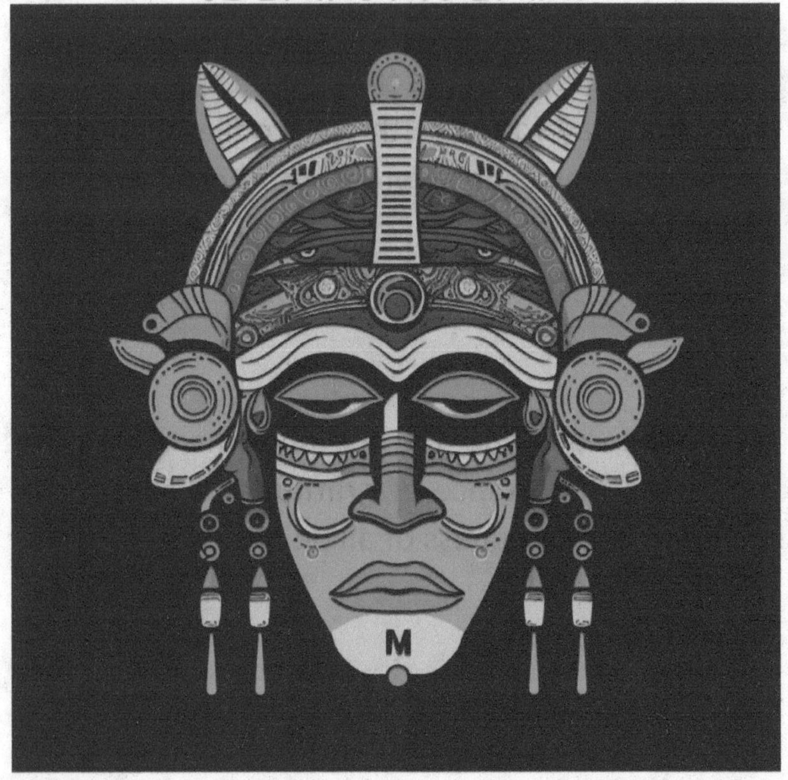

Once upon a time, in the ancient kingdom of Dahomey, nestled in the heart of Benin, there existed a land of enchantment and mystery. This land was blessed with an array of powerful deities, guardians of the people and protectors of their heritage. The story of "The Deities of Dahomey" is a captivating tale that has been passed down through generations, bringing joy and wonder to children like you.

Long, long ago, when the world was still young, the people of Dahomey believed in a pantheon of gods and goddesses who watched over their land. Each deity possessed extraordinary powers and had a unique role in shaping the lives of the people. Their stories were woven into the tapestry of Dahomey's rich culture and traditions.

In this fascinating tale, we embark on a journey to discover the magnificent deities and the significance they hold in the lives of the people. Let's meet some of them:

Mawu, the Sky Goddess: Mawu, with her radiant smile and gentle touch, was responsible for bringing light and life to the world. She painted the sky with vibrant colors and sent cool breezes to soothe the land. Her presence was a reminder of the beauty and harmony that surrounded the people.

Legba, the Messenger: Legba was a mischievous deity with a quick wit and a twinkle in his eyes. He served as the intermediary between the human realm and the spirit world, carrying messages from one to the other. His tricks and riddles kept everyone on their toes and added an element of excitement to their lives.

Aganju, the Earth Father: Aganju was a mighty deity who personified strength and fertility. With each step he took, the ground shook, and crops flourished in his wake. The people revered him for his ability to nurture the land and provide sustenance to all.

Ayida-Weddo, the Rainbow Serpent: Ayida-Weddo was a magnificent deity who traveled across the sky in vibrant arcs of color. She symbolized unity and renewal, reminding the people of the importance of embracing diversity and finding beauty in every corner of the world.

These deities, among others, played pivotal roles in the lives of the people of Dahomey. They were celebrated through joyful festivals and grand ceremonies, where their stories came to life through music, dance, and colorful costumes. The people believed that by honoring these deities, they would receive blessings, protection, and guidance. Now let's get to the story... In the kingdom of Dahomey, the people lived harmoniously, guided by the wisdom and protection of the deities. They offered prayers, performed rituals, and celebrated the gods and goddesses who watched over them. The story of "The Deities of Dahomey" begins with a time when the kingdom faced a great challenge.

A terrible drought plagued the land, and crops withered, leaving the people hungry and desperate. They turned to their deities, seeking guidance and intervention. Mawu, the Sky Goddess, heard their cries and summoned an assembly of deities to discuss the plight of the people.

Legba, the Messenger, danced with his mischievous steps and proclaimed, "We must find a way to bring rain and revive the land!" Aganju, the Earth Father, thumped his mighty staff, agreeing with a booming voice. Ayida-Weddo, the Rainbow Serpent, hissed with determination, ready to lend her colorful support.

Together, the deities devised a plan to save their beloved kingdom. Mawu called upon the spirits of the ancestors, who whispered ancient secrets to her. She then shared her divine vision with the assembly. The deities would embark on a sacred journey to a hidden lake in the heart of the wilderness, where the Rain Spirit resided.

Led by Legba, the deities set off on their quest. They trekked through dense forests, crossed mighty rivers, and braved treacherous mountain paths. Along the way, they encountered magical creatures, faced daunting challenges, and relied on their unique powers to overcome each obstacle.

Finally, after days of arduous travel, they reached the hidden lake. Its tranquil waters shimmered under the golden rays of the sun. Ayida-Weddo summoned her rainbow arcs, creating a beautiful bridge for the deities to cross. With their hearts full of hope, they ventured toward the dwelling of the Rain Spirit.

Inside the cave, they discovered a grand throne where the Rain Spirit awaited them. With a voice as soothing as a summer rain, the spirit greeted the deities and listened to their plea. Moved by their devotion and love for the people, the Rain Spirit agreed to bless the land with much-needed rain.

The deities returned to Dahomey, their hearts brimming with joy. They danced, sang, and spread the news of the Rain Spirit's benevolence. The people, filled with gratitude, joined in the celebrations, honoring the deities for their bravery and unwavering commitment to their kingdom.

<u>**Lessons**</u>

*The deities of Dahomey were revered as protectors and guardians, ensuring the prosperity and well-being of the land.

*Their stories remind many of the power of unity, faith, and the enduring bond between humans and their deities.

THE STORY OF RAMONG AND AJOK (ACHOLI, UGANDA)

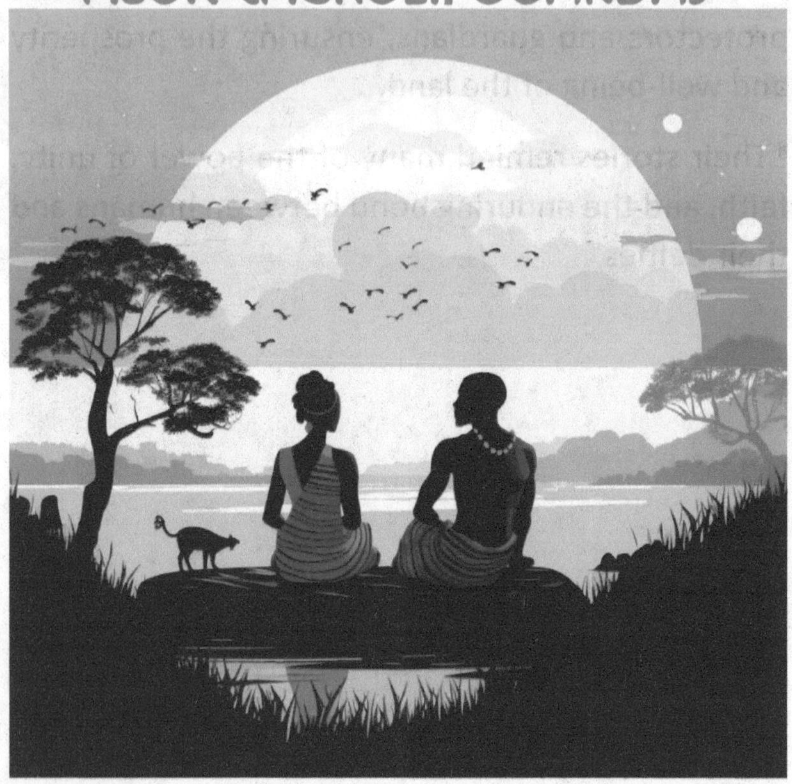

Once upon a time, in the beautiful land of Acholi, Uganda, there lived a brave and curious young boy named Ramong. He had heard whispers of an extraordinary creature called Ajok, a magnificent lion with shimmering golden fur and the wisdom of the ancient spirits.

The legend of Ramong and Ajok had been passed down through generations, enchanting children and adults alike. It is said that long ago, when the world was still young, a young Acholi warrior named Ramong discovered a wounded lion cub all alone in the vast savannah. Filled with compassion, Ramong decided to care for the cub and named him Ajok, which means "spirit" in their language.

As Ajok grew stronger and larger, he became not only Ramong's faithful companion but also his protector. They embarked on incredible adventures together, venturing deep into the heart of the Acholi kingdom. Ramong and Ajok would encounter various challenges, from treacherous rivers to cunning tricksters, but their bond remained unbreakable.

The significance of this remarkable folktale lies in its celebration of bravery, compassion, and the power of friendship. It reminds us that even the most unlikely friendships can lead to extraordinary journeys and great accomplishments. The story of Ramong and Ajok showcases the deep connection between humans and animals, emphasizing the importance of respecting and caring for the natural world.

In Acholi culture, this folktale has become beloved for its lessons on courage and unity. The Acholi people believe that the spirits of their ancestors reside in the majestic lions of the land, symbolizing strength and protection. The tale of Ramong and Ajok embodies these beliefs, inspiring young Acholi children to embrace their heritage and the wisdom of their ancestors.

Imagine, dear children, roaming the vast African plains with Ramong and Ajok by your side! Feel the warm breeze brush against your cheeks as you embark on daring quests and encounter the enchanting wildlife of Uganda. The vibrant colors of the savannah come alive as you witness the bond between a young boy and his magical lion, learning about the importance of loyalty, kindness, and bravery.

Lessons

*This tale teaches rare values such as loyalty, bravery, and kindness.

WHY THE BAT ONLY FLIES BY NIGHT (NIGERIA)

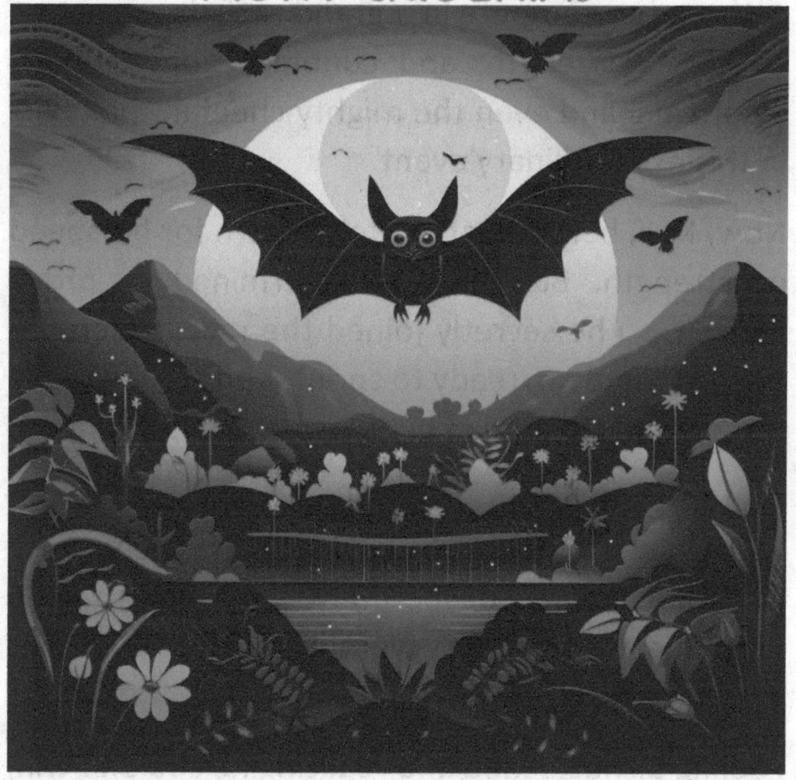

Long, long ago, in the heart of Africa, there lived a mischievous and curious little Bat named Kofi. With his sleek black wings and keen senses, Kofi could fly swiftly through the night, soaring high above the treetops. But there was a mystery surrounding Kofi, a reason why he only appeared when the moon took its place in the sky.

Legend has it that ages ago, when the world was still young, the animals of the African savannah gathered to compete in a grand race. It was a test of speed, strength, and cunning. Lions, zebras, elephants, and even the mighty cheetah took part in this extraordinary event.

Now, Kofi, being a Bat, wasn't known for his speed or strength. But he was determined to prove himself, so he secretly joined the race. When the animals lined up, ready to sprint, Kofi stood among them, ready to spread his wings and take flight.

As the race began, the animals dashed forward with thunderous strides, leaving Kofi far behind. He flapped his wings desperately, struggling to keep up. But alas, his efforts were in vain, for the other creatures were far too swift for him.

Feeling disheartened and realizing he couldn't win, Kofi devised a devious plan. As the animals neared the finish line, he swooped down and grabbed hold of the powerful Eagle's tail. With a mischievous grin, he hoped to hitch a ride and claim an undeserved victory.

But oh, what a grave mistake he made! The Eagle, being wise and strong, sensed Kofi's cunning act. In a flash of anger, he turned and confronted the Bat.

The animals gathered around, their eyes filled with disappointment and anger at Kofi's deceit.

To punish Kofi for his trickery, the animals declared that from that day forward, he would only fly during the night. They believed that the darkness would serve as a reminder of his deceitful ways and teach him a valuable lesson.

And so, ever since that fateful race, Kofi the Bat roams the nighttime skies, forever hiding from the light of day. He flies in silence, with a heavy heart, reminding himself and others that honesty and fairness should guide our actions.

<u>Lessons</u>

*The tale of "Why the Bat flies by Night" serves as a reminder of the consequences of dishonesty and the importance of integrity. *This story reveals the value of truth and the significance of owning up to our mistakes.

THE STORY OF THE APE. THE SNAKE. AND THE LION (TANZANIA)

Once upon a time, in a village called Keedeejee, nestled deep within the heart of Tanzania, there lived a young boy named Juma. Juma's mother, after the untimely passing of his father, struggled to provide enough food for them both. They lived in constant hunger, barely scraping by each day.

One day, Juma couldn't bear to see his mother suffer any longer. Determined to make a change, he approached her and said, "Mother, why are we always hungry? What work did Father do to support us?"

With a heavy heart, his mother replied, "Your father was a hunter. He set traps in the forest, and we survived on the animals he caught."

Eyes gleaming with excitement, Juma exclaimed, "That sounds like fun, not work! I want to set traps too, so we can have enough to eat."

And so, the next day, Juma ventured into the lush, mysterious forest. He gathered branches from the trees, his young hands skillfully crafting them into traps. With determination burning in his heart, he twisted coconut fibers into ropes to set up the snares.

Days turned into weeks as Juma tirelessly set trap after trap. And then, the moment arrived—his efforts bore fruit. In one of his traps, he discovered a mischievous ape caught within its grasp. The ape pleaded, "Young one, please release me! I am Nana, the ape. Spare my life, and I promise to repay your kindness when the time comes."

Intrigued by the ape's words, Juma set Nana free. Perched on a tree branch, Nana shared his wisdom with the young boy, cautioning him against the unkindness of men. He warned, "Believe me, Kofi, men are often ungrateful. Be wary of their intentions when you show them kindness."

On another fateful day, Juma stumbled upon a snake ensnared in his trap. Just as he prepared to call for help, the snake pleaded, "Wait, young one! I am Nia, the snake. Release me, and in return, I shall be your ally when you need it most."

Juma, remembering Nana's words, freed Nia. Grateful for his mercy, Nia advised Kofi to be cautious, as men often returned kindness with harm.

As fate would have it, Juma's final encounter within his traps was a mighty lion named Lulu. Trembling with fear, Juma was astonished when Lulu spoke gently, "Do not fear me, young one. I am Lemi, the very old lion. Free me from this trap, and I shall protect you when the time comes."

Placing his trust in Lemi's words, Juma released the lion. Before departing, Lemi emphasized the importance of being wary of men's actions, for they often repaid kindness with unkindness.

As Juma continued his journey, he soon found himself lost in unfamiliar territory. Weary and hungry, he contemplated giving up. But just as despair settled in, a familiar voice called out, "Juma, where are you going?"

Looking up, Juma was overjoyed to see Nana, the ape, returning his kindness. Nana scurried off to gardens nearby and returned with ripe paw-paws and bananas. He even brought a calabash filled with refreshing water. Juma savored the food and drink, reenergized by the kindness bestowed upon him.

Their paths diverged once more, and Juma continued his journey. Eventually, he encountered Lemi, the wise lion, who recognized Juma's plight.

Lemi provided him with game to satisfy his hunger, and even shared a comforting fire for warmth. Juma's spirits lifted as he felt the lion's gratitude for his earlier act of compassion.

With newfound strength and determination, Juma pressed on, hoping to find his way back home. As he walked, he stumbled upon a humble farm, where he encountered a feeble, elderly woman. She pleaded, "Stranger, my husband is gravely ill, and I seek someone who can make him a healing remedy. Will you help us?"

Juma hesitated, for he possessed no knowledge of medicine. "I am sorry, kind woman," he replied. "I am not a healer, but a hunter. I fear I cannot assist you."

As he continued his journey, Juma reached a crossroad leading to a bustling city. Nearby, he spotted a well with a bucket beside it, and a flicker of hope sparked within him. "Perhaps a drink from the well will provide me with much-needed guidance," he mused.

But as he peered into the well, his eyes widened with astonishment—for there, coiled gracefully, was Nia, the snake he had freed before. Nia's voice echoed from the depths, "Juma, wait a moment!" Slithering out, he approached Kofi and said, "Do you not recognize me? I am Nia, the snake you spared. Trust me once more, and I shall repay your kindness."

Curiosity piqued, Juma handed Nia his small bag, and to his amazement, Nia filled it with shimmering chains of gold and silver. Grateful for Nia's generosity, Kofi bid him farewell, ready to face the city's unknown challenges.

However, as Juma arrived at the city, a man whom he had previously released from a trap recognized him. Fueled by jealousy and malice, the man spread rumors, accusing Juma of being a sorcerer disguised as a young man.

Word reached the sultan, who ordered soldiers to seize Juma and his bag of chains. Fear coursed through Juma's veins as he faced the accusations. Yet, just as despair threatened to consume him, Lemi, the venerable lion, arrived, and without hesitation, placed himself at the feet of the accuser.

Witnessing this extraordinary sight, the people exclaimed, "Look! It is Lemi, the guardian of the forest, standing by Kofi's side! Surely this proves his innocence."

Realizing their grave mistake, the people untied Juma's hands and apologized for their misguided judgment. The sultan, intrigued by the tale, questioned Kofi, eager to understand the truth.

With sincerity, Juma recounted his encounters with Nana, Nia, and Lemi—their warnings, their acts of gratitude, and the lesson they imparted. The sultan listened intently, recognizing the wisdom hidden within these encounters.

Moved by the young hunter's journey, the sultan declared, "Though there may be ungrateful individuals, Juma has shown us the true essence of kindness and discernment. Let his story be a reminder that compassion should not be abandoned, even when faced with unkindness."

And so, Juma became known throughout the land for his unwavering kindness and discernment. His tale spread far and wide, becoming a cherished part of the African folklore tradition—a reminder to children of the importance of compassion and the power of discerning hearts.

Lessons

*This story is a lesson that while acts of kindness may sometimes go unnoticed or unappreciated, it is crucial to remain true to one's compassionate nature.

WHY THE TORTOISE HAS NO HAIR (SOUTH AFRICA)

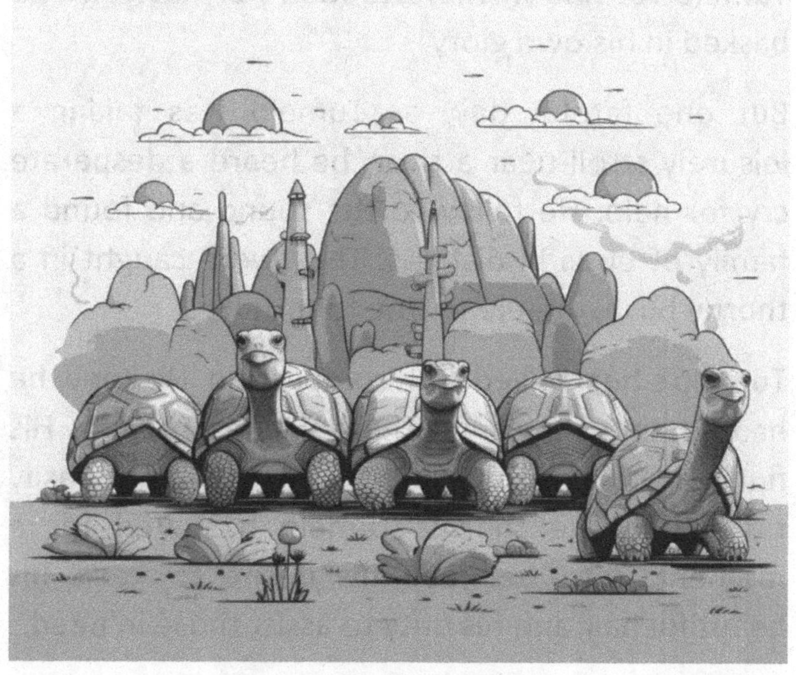

Once upon a time, in the vast plains of South Africa, there lived a tortoise named Tumelo. Tumelo was unlike any other tortoise you've ever seen. Instead of having a hard, scaly shell, he had a soft, silky covering of fluffy hair. This made him stand out from the rest of his tortoise friends, who were all smooth and shiny.

Now, Tumelo loved his hair. It made him feel unique and special. Everywhere he went, he would strut proudly, showing off his beautiful mane of silky hair. The other animals would often gather around him, admiring his distinct appearance. Tumelo reveled in the attention he received and basked in his own glory.

But one fateful day, as Tumelo was taking a leisurely stroll near a river, he heard a desperate cry for help. He followed the sound and found a family of birds in distress. They were caught in a thorny bush, unable to free themselves.

Tumelo's heart filled with compassion. He knew he had to help them, but there was a problem. His fluffy hair was so delicate that it would get easily tangled in the thorns. Tumelo hesitated for a moment, torn between his desire to keep his beautiful hair and his duty to assist those in need.

With a deep breath, Tumelo made a brave decision. He laid down next to the bush and gently rolled himself, allowing his fluffy hair to get entangled in the thorns. It was a painful sacrifice, but Tumelo endured it, knowing that he was helping the trapped birds.

The birds, now free, chirped with joy and gratitude. They sang a beautiful melody to honor Tumelo's selflessness. News of his noble act spread throughout the animal kingdom, and soon all the animals knew of the tortoise who had sacrificed his hair for the well-being of others.

From that day on, Tumelo's story became a popular folktale in South Africa. The tale of "Why the Tortoise has no Hair on" was passed down from generation to generation, reminding everyone of the importance of kindness and selflessness.

So, dear children, remember the story of Tumelo, the tortoise with the fluffy hair. Let his selflessness inspire you to be kind, compassionate, and willing to make sacrifices for the greater good. Embrace your African heritage and its rich tradition of storytelling, for within these tales lie wisdom, lessons, and the essence of who we are.

Lessons

*This enchanting folktale teaches us that true beauty lies not in our outward appearance but in the goodness of our hearts.

*Tumelo's sacrifice is a lesson that we are to help others, even if it means letting go of something dear to us.

THE HAWK AND THE OWL (NIGERIA)

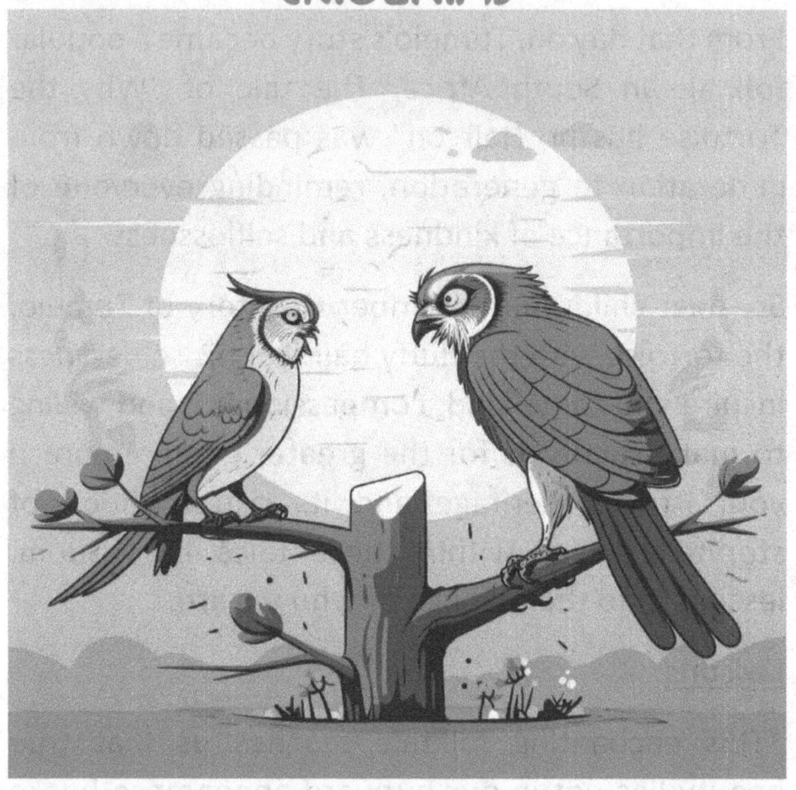

Once upon a time, in the ancient kingdom of Calabar, there lived a wise and powerful king named Effiong. He was known for his extravagant feasts, to which all the creatures of the land, air, and water were invited. Among them, the hawk was the king's most trusted messenger, thanks to his incredible speed and agility.

After serving the king faithfully for many years, the hawk began to grow old and sought retirement. He approached the king and asked what would become of him in his twilight years. The king, grateful for the hawk's loyal service, promised to provide him with a lifelong source of sustenance. He instructed the hawk to bring him any living creature, and from then on, the hawk would be allowed to feast on that specific species without worry.

Eager to secure his future, the hawk embarked on a journey across forests and fields, searching for the perfect creature to present to the king. Eventually, he came across a young and helpless owl that had fallen from its nest. The hawk knew he had found his offering and carried the owlet to the king.

Delighted by the hawk's choice, the king declared that henceforth, the hawk would feed on owls. Excitedly, the hawk flew back to his friends and shared the news. However, one wise bird among them cautioned the hawk, asking him what the parents of the owl had done when their child was taken away.

The hawk, puzzled, replied that the owl parents had remained silent and made no attempt to rescue their owlet. Sensing danger, the wise bird advised the hawk to return the owlet to its parents. After all, he reasoned, the owl parents' silence might indicate a hidden plan for vengeance that could strike during the night.

Taking the advice to heart, the hawk flew back to the owl's nest and gently placed the owlet near its parents. Relieved, he sought another creature to fulfill the king's demand. However, as news spread that the hawk had seized an owl, the other birds became cautious, hiding themselves whenever the hawk approached. This made it impossible for the hawk to catch any of them.

Disheartened, the hawk started to fly home when he spotted a flock of chickens near a house. The chickens were happily pecking at the ground, with little chicks darting around under the watchful eye of a protective mother hen. The hawk saw an opportunity and swooped down, seizing the smallest chicken in his strong claws.

Instantly, chaos erupted among the chickens. The roosters crowed loudly, and the mother hen desperately tried to rescue her precious chick, fluffing up her feathers and making daring attempts to reclaim her little one. But the hawk managed to carry the chicken away. Frightened, the fowls and chicks scattered, seeking refuge in bushes and hiding places.

Proudly, the hawk presented the chicken to the king, explaining that he had returned the owl to its parents, realizing he had no desire to harm it. The king, impressed by the hawk's compassion, declared that from that day forward, the hawk could feast on chickens.

Returning to his nest, the hawk excitedly shared the story with his wise friend. The friend inquired about the reaction of the chicken's parents when their child was snatched away. The hawk recounted the commotion and noise they made but assured his friend that nothing more had transpired.

With a knowing smile, the wise friend reassured the hawk that he could safely devour chickens. Those who made a ruckus during the day, he explained, would fall into deep slumber at night and pose no threat. It was those who remained silent when injured or wronged that one should truly fear, for their silence masked their plotting and mischief-making under the cover of darkness.

And so, the hawk continued to enjoy his newfound delicacy of chickens, relishing each meal without worry. As the days turned into nights, he would soar through the moonlit sky, his belly full and his heart content.

Lessons

*The tale of "The Hawk and the Owl" teaches a valuable lesson about trust, wisdom, and the importance of paying attention to the subtle cues of nature.

THE ORPHAN BOY AND THE MAGIC STONE (NIGERIA)

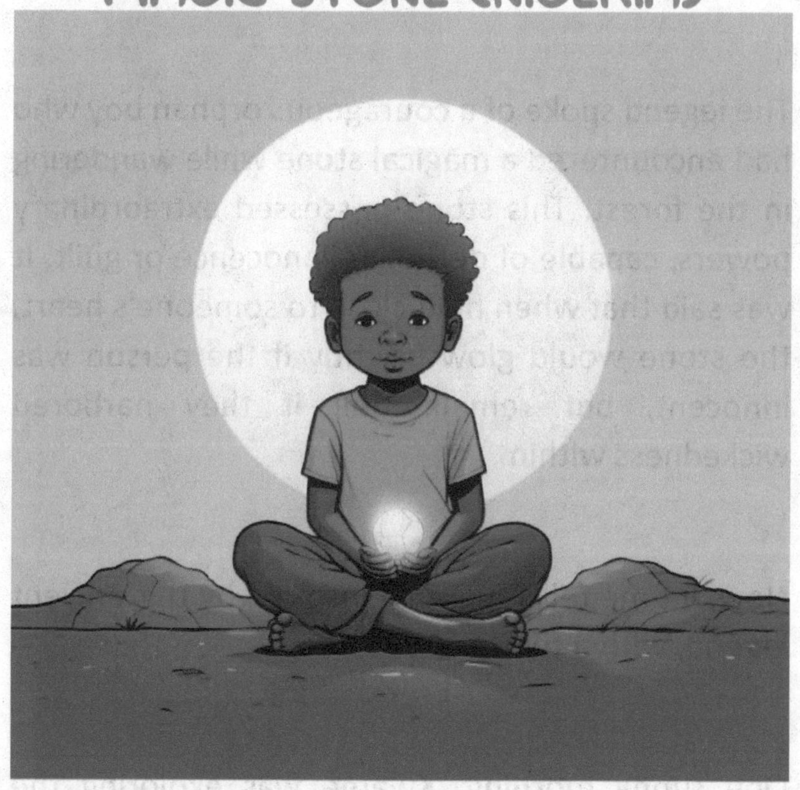

Long ago, during a time when witches roamed the land, the village was plagued by fear and suspicion. Whenever anyone was accused of being a witch, they were subjected to a terrifying ordeal called the "Esere Bean Trial." The Esere bean was a poisonous seed, and if someone accused of witchcraft could not vomit after consuming it, they would suffer a painful death. However, if they managed to vomit, they would be declared innocent and spared from this dreadful fate.

The legend spoke of a courageous orphan boy who had encountered a magical stone while wandering in the forest. This stone possessed extraordinary powers, capable of detecting innocence or guilt. It was said that when held close to someone's heart, the stone would glow brightly if the person was innocent, but remain dull if they harbored wickedness within.

Now, let me tell you a tale inspired by this ancient legend, with a twist of my own.

One sunny morning, Kwame was exploring the enchanting forest near his village when he stumbled upon a sparkling stone nestled beneath a majestic baobab tree. As he picked up the stone, a warm glow enveloped his hand, filling his heart with courage and curiosity.

Little did he know that this stone was no ordinary pebble. It was the legendary Magic Stone, awakened by Kwame's pure heart and destined to help him bring justice and harmony to his village.

Word spread quickly throughout the village about the brave orphan boy who had discovered the Magic Stone. People came from far and wide, seeking Kwame's assistance in uncovering the truth behind accusations of witchcraft.

With the Magic Stone in his possession, Kwame became a beacon of hope and fairness. He would carefully examine the accused, holding the stone close to their hearts. And as the stone shimmered with a radiant light, the truth would be revealed.

One day, an elderly woman named Ama was accused of practicing dark magic. The village was divided, and Ama's life hung in the balance. Kwame, with his unwavering determination, came forward to aid Ama in her time of need.

As the villagers gathered, Kwame approached Ama with a gentle smile. He held the Magic Stone close to her heart, and to everyone's amazement, it gleamed brightly, casting a golden glow upon them. The truth was unveiled for all to see — Ama was innocent.

The villagers gasped in astonishment, realizing the power of the Magic Stone and the injustice they had almost committed. From that day forward, the villagers abandoned the cruel Esere Bean Trial and embraced the fair judgment brought by the Magic Stone.

Kwame's selflessness and his ability to discern truth from falsehood earned him the admiration and respect of the entire village. He became a hero, not only for bringing justice but also for reminding the people of the importance of compassion and understanding.

And so, the legend of "The Orphan Boy and the Magic Stone" continued to be told throughout generations. It became a symbol of courage, fairness, and the triumph of kindness over fear.

Lessons

*This tale is a constant reminder to always seek the truth and treat others with compassion, for it is in our hands to create a world where fairness and understanding prevail.

CONCLUSION

And so, dear young readers, our grand adventure through the captivating African folklore comes to a close. We hope that these tales have ignited your imagination, transported you to distant lands, and filled your hearts with a sense of wonder.

As you turn the final page of this book, remember that these stories are not just stories. They are a tapestry of heritage, a legacy of wisdom passed down through generations. They remind us of the power of storytelling, the strength of community, and the importance of embracing our roots.

Take these tales with you, carry them in your hearts, and let them inspire you to be brave, kind, and curious. Just like the heroes and heroines you've met within these pages, may you find the courage to face challenges, the wisdom to make the right choices, and the compassion to create a world filled with understanding and unity.

Your African heritage is a gift, a treasure waiting to be explored. The stories of the past hold within them the seeds of the future, and you, dear reader, are an integral part of this beautiful tapestry.

As you journey through life, may the spirit of Africa guide you, and may the magic of these stories stay with you forever. Remember, the power of storytelling lies not only in the tales themselves but also in the way they shape who we are and how we see the world.

Farewell, young adventurers, but remember, this is not the end. It is merely the beginning of your own extraordinary story, one that you will continue to write with each step you take. May the spirit of Africa forever shine brightly within you.